LAWYERS
THE RULE OF LAW
AND LIBERALISM
IN MODERN EGYPT

HOOVER INSTITUTION PUBLICATIONS

lawyers the rule of law and liberalism in modern Egypt

FARHAT J. ZIADEH

HOOVER INSTITUTION ON WAR, REVOLUTION AND PEACE
Stanford University, Stanford California 1968

The Hoover Institution on War, Revolution and Peace, founded at Stanford University in 1919 by the late President Herbert Hoover, is a center for advanced study and research on public and international affairs in the twentieth century. The views expressed in its publications are entirely those of the authors and do not necessarily reflect the views of the Hoover Institution.

Hoover Institution Publications 75

Library of Congress Catalog Card Number: 68–9503
Printed in the United States of America

To Shireen, Susan, Rhonda, Deena, and Reema

preface

This monograph traces the rise of Western-oriented lawyers in Egypt to a position of dominance in public life until the army revolt of 1952, when fundamental changes in power alignment relegated them to the modest role of legal technicians. A detailed consideration of their position and status after 1952 falls outside the scope of this work, and the brief discussion in Chapter Seven is intended only to show their complete eclipse as a powerful national force.

As indicated in Chapter One, except for the *sharīʿah*—that idealistic system of law in Islam which theoretically limited the executive power—there was very little in the Islamic background of Egypt that was conducive to the rise of constitutionality and a rule of law. The reforms introduced by the rulers of Egypt during the first, second, and third quarters of the nineteenth century, particularly in the matter of secularizing some aspects of law and state machinery, marked the inception of modern legal thinking and the spread of legal knowledge concerning rights, duties, freedoms, and remedies. This was not a deliberate development of a rule of law, for local rulers still dominated all judicial tribunals, but the legal concepts and doctrines they had set in motion through their reforms prepared the way for the emergence of the mixed courts and, later, the national courts (Chapter Two). These new tribunals enabled foreign lawyers and some European-trained Egyptian lawyers to develop and strengthen these concepts further, until a genuine rule of law, replacing the arbitrary actions of khedives and administrators, was established in the country. The stage was now set for the rise of a new class of Egyptian lawyers and the development of a legal profession (Chapter Three) that participated in the elucidation and application of the concepts, procedures, and remedies of the rule of law and whose existence and interests depended upon the spread of the rule of law and its many ramifications.

By the nature of their profession lawyers became public figures, addressing themselves to public issues. The first such issue was nationalist action for Egypt's complete independence and the development of constitutional government (Chapter Four). The quasi-monopoly of the legal profession on this issue resulted from the failure of the old military and Azharite leadership and the fact that internationalization of the Egyptian question following the British occupation required a leadership capable of conducting the Egyptian case within the context of world politics. Further, because of their involvement in matters of constitutionality, rule of law, and progressive legislation, Egyptian lawyers loomed large in the eyes of the public as the champions of these concepts, thus enhancing not only their leadership, but their reputation as advocates of liberal and progressive causes (Chapter Five).

In addressing themselves to national problems, both individually and as a group, lawyers took a liberal and progressive position. Nowhere was this more evident than in the crucial question of legal reform (Chapter Six), where they endeavored to destroy the strongholds of judicial privilege and effect reforms in matters of personal status, charitable and family *waqfs*, and civil law without seriously violating the religious sensibilities of traditional elements.

The monolithic character of the military regime after 1952 put an end to the lawyers' position of dominance in public life and almost completely stifled their prestige and influence (Chapter Seven). Nevertheless, the rule of law they helped to establish continues to be the guiding spirit of Egyptian courts, at least for nonpolitical cases,[1] and the ideas on legal reform they had advanced became the basis of many measures carried through by the new regime.

Some explanation of the sources for this book is in order here. Discussions of the modernization of the Egyptian state and law under Muḥammad 'Ali and his successors are based on works by Fatḥi Zaghlūl and 'Azīz Khānki, both of whom had made extensive use of 'Ābidīn archives. At the time the research for this monograph was conducted, the 'Ābidīn archives were closed to the public. The two-volume *Minutes of the General Assembly of the National Bar Association*, which were consulted extensively for the development of the legal profession, were handwritten in ledger-type books with pages numbered from left to right in the European manner. However, since the minutes were kept in Arabic and thus proceeded from the right to left, the pagination is in descending order; hence the descending order in the pagination of quotations. The minutes of the Sharī'ah Bar Association were consulted at the Ministry of Finance in Cairo, where the records of that defunct association are kept, and the British Foreign Office documents cited were consulted at the Public Record Office in London.

The list of friends who helped in one way or another is too long to set out here; this, however, does not detract from my indebtedness to every one of them. Special mention must be made of the help received from Prof. H. A. R. Gibb, who suggested the writing of this book; from Prof. Morroe Berger, Director of the Program in Near Eastern Studies at Princeton University; from Profs. Manfred Halpern, Albert Hourani, and John Mikhail, who read the entire manuscript; from 'Abd al-Raḥmān al-Rāfi'i, the Egyptian lawyer-historian, Dr. 'Abd al-Razzāq al-Sanhūri, Dr. Muḥammad Kāmil Malash, Mr. Aḥmad Ṣafwat, Shaykh Muḥammad Abu Zahrah, Dr. Bayard Dodge, and Judge J. Y. Brinton in facilitating my research in Cairo; and from John Douw, Dr. Richard Debs, and Dr. David Partington in research and

[1] Interview with 'Abd al-Razzāq al-Sanhūri in March, 1962.

bibligraphy. I should also like to thank Prof. T. Cuyler Young, Chairman of the Department of Oriental Studies, Princeton University, for his interest, and the Program in Near Eastern Studies at Princeton for financial support during my research in Egypt. Finally, thanks are due to Howard Koch, Dr. George Rentz, and the staff of the Hoover Institution for making the publication of this work possible. I am particularly indebted to Dr. Rentz and Nancy Clark for their most meticulous review of the manuscript and for their numerous emendations.

F. J. Ziadeh

contents

LAWYERS
THE RULE OF LAW
AND LIBERALISM
IN MODERN EGYPT

CHAPTER ONE

the secularization of state and law

THE ISLAMIC BACKGROUND

There was very little in the course of Egyptian history from the early Islamic period up to the accession of Ismāʿīl Pasha in 1863 that was conducive to the emergence of an independent legal system with a vigorous body of men capable of establishing and maintaining a rule of law. It is true that the *ulema,* or religious scholars, considered themselves the guardians and interpreters of the *sharīʿah,* that sacred and eternal law which "is suitable for every time and clime" and which limits both the individual and the ruler. It is also true that they were the only type of "nobility" not completely dependent upon the prince and were therefore in a position, if they so desired, to protest his irregular acts or even to apply a brake to his absolute power. However, two factors militated against the emergence of the *ulema* as the guardians of a rule of law. In the first place, the *sharī'ah* was looked upon as an ideal system for an ideal Muslim state[1] and was therefore to a large extent divorced from the practical necessities of daily life. The result was that the *sharī'ah* and those who applied it lost to the agents of the prince control over both criminal and commercial law and were thus confined to civil cases and questions of personal status. In the second place, throughout Islamic history the judiciary, composed in the main of *ulema,* performed their functions as a result of delegation by the executive and were therefore dependent upon it. Such a situation could hardly be favorable for the emergence of an independent body capable of maintaining a rule of law.

Even in their small bailiwick, the *sharī'ah* judges were not entirely without interference. Beginning with the rule of the Mamlūk sultan Baybars, from 1260 to 1277, the four *sharī'ah* chief justices, representing the four *sunni,* or orthodox rites—Ḥanafi, Māliki, Shāfi'i, and Ḥanbali—seemed to have enjoyed a fairly stable and well-defined jurisdiction, free on the whole from the active interference by the prince or his agents. However, with the Ottoman conquest in 1517, and the resultant upheaval, the picture changed. The inertia that had prevailed in judicial affairs gave way to an order in which the executive arm interfered to correct abuses and to reorganize the whole system. In the first year of the conquest the Ottoman sultan Selim I, while still in Egypt, personally beat a judge, made him wear the uncleaned stomach of an ox as a hat, and caused him to be paraded in the streets of Cairo riding backward on a donkey to bring him into ridicule and contempt. The reason, as stated by the historian Ibn

[1] N. J. Coulson, Doctrine and Practice in Islamic Law, *Bulletin of the School of Oriental and African Studies,* vol. 18, part 2, 1956.

Iyās,[2] was that the judge had performed a marriage ceremony between an Ottoman soldier and a Mamlūk widow who, unknown to the judge, had not completed her *'iddah,* or period of retirement before remarriage. A more likely reason may have been that Selim had absolutely prohibited the marriage of Ottoman soldiers to widows of Mamlūk soldiers who had died in the war and the judges had disregarded his orders.

Selim began his reorganization of the judicial system by appointing an Ottoman judge to supervise the activities of the Egyptian judges. Then his governor, Khāyir Bey, decreed that the four chief justices should reduce the number of lieutenant judges and dismiss the *wukalā',* or advocates, and various messengers loitering at their doors. As a further "reform," an Ottoman military commander, surrounded by a group of janissaries (a special corps of soldiers), inaugurated the practice of sitting on an elevated platform in front of the Ṣāliḥiyyah school, the headquarters of the Ottoman chief judge in Cairo, and exacting six *dirhems* from both the plaintiff and the defendant in every judicial matter to be tried by any *sharī'ah* judge. His authority must have been so overwhelming that "no judge dared oppose him; he even claimed that he was superior to judges in *sharī'ah* matters, and used to beat or imprison those deserving to be beaten or imprisoned without reference to the judges."[3]

More far-reaching changes in the judicial system were introduced a few years later during the reign of Sulaymān. In 1521–1522 (the year 928 A.H.)[4] this sultan appointed a *qāḍi*

[2] Muḥammad Ibn Aḥmad Ibn Iyās, *Badā'i' al-Zuhūr,* vol. III, Būlāq, 1311–1312 A.H., p. 120.

[3] Ibn Iyās, pp. 150, 156.

[4] The era of *anno hegira* (A.H.)., as established by the second caliph, 'Umar, began at sunset on July 15, 622 A.D., the date of Muhammad's *hegira* (*hijrah,* flight) from Mecca to Medina to escape persecution. The Muslim year is a lunar year of 354 days (or 355 days every eleven years in a cycle of thirty). Hence a *hegira* century corresponds approximately to ninety-seven years in the Gregorian calendar.

'askar, or chief judge,[5] to replace the four chief justices and to carry on the judicial process according to the four *sunni* rites. He was to have only four lieutenant judges, one of each rite. No one was to conclude a contract, or create a *waqf* endowment (dedication of property in perpetuity), or perform any *sharī'ah* act without referring the matter to the *qāḍi 'askar.*[6]

This constant interference by the executive power in the work of the *sharī'ah* judges was not conducive to the emergence of a rule of law, nor were the court abuses that the interference was intended to correct.[7] The only element that could be construed as contributing toward this end was the willingness of some *sharī'ah* judges to apply the strict rules of the *sharī'ah* regardless of the displeasure of the authorities or even of the ignorant general public. This deference to right conduct, to a semblance of a rule of law, must be attributed to the hold the *sharī'ah* had over those judges and the *ulema* in general.[8]

[5] As the name indicates, this official was originally the chief military judge, but long before Ottoman times he had acquired a civilian character as chief judge of a country or province.

[6] Ibn Iyās, p. 296.

[7] See, for example, Ibn Iyās, p. 273.

[8] This deference to right conduct is vividly illustrated by an incident recorded by Ibn Iyās. During the reign of Sulaymān, and before the reorganization of the judicial system, three Copts (Egyptian Christians) witnessing some festivity at the home of a Ḥanafi lieutenant judge became inebriated and offensive in their behavior. The host asked them in strong language to desist. They retorted in kind and, it was said, cursed the Islamic religion, a charge meriting death according to the *sharī'ah.* Accordingly, he had them arrested and sent to the headquarters of the four chief justices for trial. The Māliki chief justice was convinced of their guilt, but because of the extenuating cirumstance of drunkenness, instead of sentencing them to death, he ordered that they be whipped, the prescribed punishment for drunkenness. The other three justices concurred in this sentence, but the complaining Ḥanafi lieutenant judge and a boisterous crowd that had gathered disagreed violently with the light sentence, and the crowd moved to have the four chief justices killed by stoning. Some janissaries seized the Copts and took them outside the court, where they cut them to pieces before turning them over to the crowd for

This state of *sharī'ah* jurisdiction continued with little change until the Napoleonic invasion of 1798, except for the fact that along the way the Ḥanafi rite became the only one applied by the *sharī'ah* courts.[9]

The *sharī'ah* courts were, of course, not the only judiciary functioning in Egypt. *Sharī'ah* judges throughout the Islamic world had already lost whatever jurisdiction they had over criminal and commercial matters to the executive authorities or their agents.[10] When the Ottoman governor of Egypt began, immediately following the Ottoman invasion, to sit every Saturday to deal with criminal cases, arbitrarily and in complete violation of the religious law,[11] he was following a well-established precedent.[12] Thus secularization of the legal system in Egypt, which started in 1798 with the French invasion and continued under Muḥammad 'Ali and his successors, had its roots deeply embedded in Islamic history.

As a background to the transformation that took place later in the legal profession and prepared the way for the emergence of lawyers as a dominant element in Egypt let us consider briefly the state of the judicial institution in the late eighteenth century, toward the end of the Ottoman period. Political power in Egypt had reverted back to the Mamlūk princes whose forebears had been defeated by the Ottomans. The administration of justice, however, continued to be the

burning. Ibn Iyās, in commenting upon this incident, said: "The crowd wanted to stone the judges. They killed these Christians and burnt them without a sentence by a judge, nor was the sentence of death applicable according to the *sharī'ah.* The crowd did this out of ignorance and aggressiveness." See Ibn Iyās, p. 268.

[9] For a description of the legal system at the time of the Napoleonic invasion see *Description de l'Égypte,* vol. XVIII, Paris, 1826, pp. 229–242.

[10] See E. Tyan, *L'Organisation judiciaire en pays d'Islam,* vol. II, Paris, 1938–1943, pp. 352–485.

[11] Ibn Iyās, p. 232.

[12] See 'Abd al-Wahhāb Ibn 'Ali al-Subki, *Mu'īd al-Ni'am* (ed. by D. W. Wyhrman), London, 1908, p. 57.

responsibility of Constantinople, for in the administration of justice "there is nothing which can encroach upon their [the Mamlūks'] political power; they bear willingly the men the Sultan sends for the difficult task of enforcing the laws. It is a difficulty which he spares them."[13] This accidental division of power should have led to the emergence of an independent judiciary capable of establishing a rule of law. However, such was not the case, for a variety of reasons, chief among which were corruption, sale of offices, and short tenure.

The *qāḍi 'askar* and the thirty-five other *qāḍis* appointed by Constantinople were for the most part unfamiliar with the language of the country; they were "assisted by dragomen who would read the pleadings, translate them to their liking and exact from the parties arbitrary costs." Tenure in office rarely exceeded two years, and very often a *qāḍi* left after only a year of duty. The *qāḍi 'askar* himself would usually remain in office for a year and a day, but the new arrival from Constantinople often sold to his predecessor his title and function, and thus a *qāḍi 'askar* might in fact remain in office for four or five years. When he was replaced, the subordinate *qāḍis* bought from his successor confirmation of their posts.[14] The *Description de L'Egypte* summed up the situation as follows:[15]

> In effect, foreign judges, ignorant for the most part of the language of the country where they go to decide the fortune, honor and life of the citizens, are not prompted by any of the sentiments which determine the integrity of magistrates: those considerations of country and fellow-citizenship, always so powerful in the hearts, do not exist at all for them. Pouring gold in full hands in order to sit in a tribunal, they regard the sword with which the law arms them only as an instrument of wealth. . . . All the means available to them are, so to speak, directed toward one goal, that of hoarding.

[13] *Description,* p. 229.
[14] *Description,* pp. 231, 232.
[15] *Description,* p. 239.

It is only fair to point out some of the brighter sides of this picture. Although *sharī'ah* law did not provide for appeal of the decision of a judge, in serious cases the *qāḍi* consulted a council of jurists. Moreover, parties were always able to obtain legal opinions of persuasive value from the *muftis,* or jurisconsults. Often such legal opinions were given even after a decision had been handed down, and if the *muftis* of the four rites agreed upon an opinion different from that of the *qāḍi,* the *qāḍi* would reconsider his judgment. The decisions of lieutenant judges, although not appealable either, were often subject to a quasi-appeal, particularly in measures against debtors and in alimony payable to wives. Cases of this kind were taken in succession from one lieutenant judge to another, until the *qāḍi* took cognizance of the matter and adjudicated it himself.[16]

In one fashion or another, then, the *qāḍis* "nearly always obtained the assent of intelligent men, and it would be unjust to apply to these magistrates, in all its severity, the reproach of partiality and corruption. . . . It is only in the case where the text of the law is obscure and open to different interpretations, or even contradictory, that the *qāḍi* dare pronounce a judgment in a manner little conforming to the spirit of the law."[17] There were often abuses in the assessment of costs, but not violation of the substantive law. In Cairo itself, the personal qualities of the *qāḍi 'askar,* as well as the surveillance exercised by the *ulema,* and even by the Mamlūk government, afforded protection from some of the abuses.

After the French invasion of 1798 the French occupation forces tried to destroy the sources of corruption without disturbing the traditional setup of the *sharī'ah* courts. When the Ottoman *qāḍi 'Askar* fled the country they appointed in his place a local *qāḍi,* Aḥmad al-'Arīshi, who continued in office (with a slight interruption) until the end of the occupation in 1801.[18]

[16] *Description,* pp. 233, 236.

[17] *Description,* p. 240.

[18] *Description,* p. 238. For a biography of al-'Arīshi see 'Abd al-Raḥmān al-Jabarti, *'Ajā'ib al-Āthār,* vol. III, Būlāq, 1297 A.H., p. 289.

They further put an end to the abuses in judicial costs by limiting them to 2 percent of the value of the claim; the amounts collected were to be divided between the *qāḍi* and the clerks of the court.

The reform that was a complete innovation and set the pattern for later reforms by Muḥammad 'Ali and his successors in the field of judicial organization was the establishment by the French in 1799 of a commercial court, Maḥkamat al-Qaḍāya. This court consisted of six Coptic and six Muslim merchants under the presidency of a Copt who had been the clerk of the *defterdār* (keeper of records). It was to adjudicate cases involving commercial matters, inheritance, and civil claims. The historian al-Jabarti, himself a member of the *ulema*, expressed his ire in calling this court "an evil innovation." He ridiculed its rules, which were widely distributed and posted in public places, as "provisos which contain other provisos written in weak and prosaic expressions which yield the meaning only after much effort because of their [members of the court] lack of knowledge of the rules of Arabic construction."[19] Al-Jabarti viewed the whole effort as a way to trick the people out of their money, with specific reference to the fees paid to this court for some of the administrative duties assigned to it, such as registration of titles to land, granting permission to travel, and registration of births.

THE EARLY COURTS

As we have seen, the Islamic background of Egypt up to the end of the Ottoman period provided little that could be construed as contributing to the emergence of a rule of law, an independent judiciary, and a viable legal system and profession. With the advent of the rule of Muḥammad 'Ali in 1805 there was a resurgence of activity in the legal and judicial field as a part of the general secularization and modernization of the state machinery. The constant reorganization of the judicial organs under Muḥammad 'Ali and his successors, plus the myriad

[19] Al-Jabarti, p. 19.

legislative measures touching every phase of life, created the sort of atmosphere in which people became aware of their rights and duties and in which legal knowledge became widespread, a *sine qua non* for an efficient and equitable legal system. Nevertheless, the absolute will of the ruler and his lieutenants, the perpetual change in judicial institutions and procedures, and the complete dependence of these procedures on the mere whim of the ruler severely retarded the emergence of an actual rule of law. This period may, however, be considered as one of preparation for such a system.

Upon assuming power in Egypt Muḥammad 'Ali hastened to discard the old Ottoman system of administration and to institute in its place his own brand. This consisted, in the main, of a council called Dīwān al-Wāli, the Governor's Council—later known as al-Majlis al-'Āli al-Malaki, the High Royal Council—which was charged with controlling the city of Cairo and settling disputes among both natives and foreigners. Four *ulema*, representing the four orthodox rites, were included in the council, which was also to deal with cases of inheritance, guardianship, and felonies. In addition to these functions, the council was charged with promulgating the laws and regulations needed in the country.[20] A more thorough mixture of executive, judicial, and legislative functions could hardly be imagined.

Laws and regulations multiplied to such an extent that they had to be unified in a new code entitled *al-Muntakhabāt* (selections), published in 1829–1830 (1245 A.H.). In the same year a law entitled Qānūn al-Fallāḥ (or al-Filāḥah), the Peasants' Law, was issued. This law was aimed at the backbone of the country, the peasant, and his relations to his fellow peasants and to government. Punishments were specified for such matters as usurpation of land, changing boundaries, conversion of beasts of burden, and theft of fruits and produce, as well as for persons not heeding conscription calls, village headmen who maltreated peasants when collecting taxes, wrongdoers who breached canals,

[20] Aḥmad Fatḥi Zaghlūl, *al-Muḥāmāh*, Cairo, 1900, p. 159; 'Azīz Khānki, *al-Tashrī 'wa-al-Qaḍā'*, Cairo, n.d., p. 2.

burned grain at threshing floors, or uttered lies to the agents of government, and notables in the country who seduced virgins.[21]

Two councils similar in function to Dīwān al-Wāli were created in Alexandria in 1830–1831 (1246 A.H.) and Damietta in 1831–1832 (1247 A.H.). A fourth council established in Jidda ceased functioning when that territory returned to Ottoman jurisdiction.[22]

A host of other councils and bureaus cropped up, each dealing with a particular service or function, such as the army, navy, finance, schools, government buildings and factories, and health and quarantine. However, those in charge, mostly the new crop of officers who had defeated the previous Mamlūk rulers, were rough and inexperienced; they oppressed the people and were concerned primarily with their own luxuries and pleasures, thus vitiating whatever good was intended by the various laws and regulations.

Muḥammad 'Ali attempted to remedy the situation by a sweeping reorganization; the result was an all-inclusive law entitled Siyāsat Nāmeh, or Constitutional Rescript,[23] issued in Rabī' I, 1253 A.H. (1837). This new law set up seven different *dīwāns* to administer the country. The first, al-Dīwān al-'Āli, the Sublime Council, was concerned, among other things, with

[21] Zaghlūl, p. 203; Khānki, p. 2. Gabriel Baer, in his article Tanzimat in Egypt: The Penal Code, *Bulletin of the School of Oriental and African Studies,* vol. 26, part I, 1963, pp. 29–49, assigns the date of the al-Muntakhabāt code to 1261 A.H. (1845) (see p. 31). Since the code referred to by Baer describes itself at the end as al-Qānūn al-Muntakhab al-Jadīd (the New Selected Code), it would seem that it was a revised version of the earlier code of 1245 A.H. (1829–1830).

[22] Zaghlūl, p. 165. In 1818 Ibrāhīm Pasha, son of Muḥammad 'Ali, completely defeated the Saudi-Wahhābi forces which had occupied the Hejaz and wrested it from Ottoman rule. The Egyptian forces, which had invaded the Hejaz in 1811, withdrew from Arabia and returned it to Ottoman jurisdiction following the Treaty of London in 1840.

[23] For the text of the preamble and the provisions of this law see Zaghlūl, pp. 171–181.

settling disputes, with *waqf* questions, and with the councils of local and European merchants. As with its predecessor, Dīwān al-Wāli, there was no distinction between judicial functions and those that were purely administrative. The six other dīwāns were those of revenue, army, navy, schools, European and Egyptian commercial affairs, and factories. In addition, two deliberative bodies were created. The first, a general assembly known as Majlis al-Mashūrah, the Consultative Council, consisting of the directors of the *dīwāns* and some notables, met once a year to deal with great issues and questions of general interest. The second, known as al-Shūra al-Khuṣūṣiyyah, Special Consultative Council, consisted of "capable persons chosen from among those slaves [subjects] who are experienced and possess the acceptability, decorum and understanding desired by the Pasha in accordance with the practice current in Europe." Its function consisted, in the main, of reviewing the reports of the *dīwāns* and passing their contents on to the Pasha, and formulating and applying the necessary rules for the employees of those *dīwāns*.

Al-Shūra al-Khuṣūṣiyyah could not carry out the tasks assigned to it, however, because its members were engaged in other functions. In 1842 Muḥammad 'Ali therefore created another council called Jam'iyyat al-Ḥaqqāniyyah, the Council of Justice, and prescribed that its members have no other duties. According to the order which created it, this council was to look into the penalties prescribed for the land and sea forces as well as for the civilian employees of the *dīwāns*. Since the council was to look into "all *siyāsiyyah* rules" (those pertaining to the discipline and punishment of state servants) an inquiry was to be made "about the practices current in Europe in this field."[24] The council consisted of a president, two army officers, two navy officers, and two civilian officers. A number of other officers were later attached to it to investigate cases.

The formation of Jam'iyyat al-Ḥaqqāniyah seems to have sparked the formation of other judicial bodies. In 1845 a council of merchants was created in Alexandria to deal with commer-

[24] Order 338 for the year 1842, quoted in Zaghlūl, pp. 182–184.

cial cases, including those involving Europeans. It was composed of a president, a deputy, a chief clerk, a clerk who spoke both Arabic and Italian, and eight elected merchants, five Egyptian and three European. In the following year a similar council was formed in Cairo with the same composition and jurisdiction. It is noteworthy that the law which set up these councils allowed in specified cases some measure of representation in actions, a step which preceded the profession of advocacy in Egypt.[25] Then, in 1855–1856 (1272 A.H.), the consuls of the various powers in Egypt approached the Egyptian government for the formation of councils of appeal for commercial cases in both Alexandria and Cairo, a request which was granted that year.[26] Each council was to be composed of two Egyptian and two European merchants, with the modern-sounding procedure of appeal set out in the law which created them and in an amendment the following year. The substantive law applied in the councils was the Ottoman Commercial Code of 1850, supplemented by French law. Appeal from the council of merchants in Alexandria lay with the council of appeal in Cairo, and appeal from the council of merchants in Cairo lay with the council of appeal in Alexandria.

Many further administrative changes took place,[27] among which was the reorganization in 1848–1849 (1265 A.H.) of Jam'iyyat al-Ḥaqqāniyyah, renamed Majlis al-Aḥkām, the Judicial Council. In addition to enlarging its membership to nine officers and adding two *ulema,* one Ḥanafi and the other Shāfi'i, to its quorum, the reorganization plan transferred summary proceedings to the administrative officers in the provinces, a step which led in 1851–1852 (1268 A.H.) to the creation of judicial councils in the provinces. There were five such councils, four in Egypt proper and one in Khartoum. Each was composed of a

[25] Zaghlūl, pp. 185–187.

[26] Register of orders for the year 1272, as quoted in Zaghlūl, pp. 187–190.

[27] For these changes see Zaghlūl, pp. 191–192.

president, four members, and four clerks. To each council were attached two *ulema,* one Ḥanafi and the other Shāfi'i, as *muftis,* or jurisconsults, on matters of Islamic law, and two notables from the province in which the council was located. The jurisdiction of these councils apparently embraced those criminal matters that had been left to the administrative officers in the provinces; purely civil matters continued to be under the jurisdiction of the *sharī'ah* courts. The councils' judgments were executed by the office of the chief executive officer, the ketkhuda.[28]

On the face of it the country seemed to be enjoying a fairly stable and smooth-running legal system. The whole system was, however, dependent upon the caprice of the Khedive. On trivial pretexts Sa'īd Pasha abolished Majlis al-Aḥkām in 1854–1855 (1271 A.H.); reinstated it in 1856–1857 (1273 A.H.); abolished it again in 1859–1860 (1276 A.H.), together with the councils of merchants in Cairo and Alexandria and the provincial judicial councils, because of a suspicion of bribery; and finally called it back to life in 1860–1861 (1277 A.H.).[29] In this atmosphere of confusion and uncertainty it is hardly necessary to point out the harm that befell the interests of litigants.

In 1861, a year after Sā'id Pasha finally reinstated Majlis al-Aḥkām, a council called the Cairo Commission was established. This body, like the commercial councils of Alexandria and Cairo, was composed of both Egyptian and European judges and dealt with issues in which foreigners were involved. Such matters had previously been handled by the administrative officers, but the rapid increase in the number of foreign residents had made additional facilities imperative. The composition of the commission reflected that of the foreign community; besides its Egyptian president and two Egyptian members it included a Greek, another European, a Jew, and an Armenian. Its jurisdiction was over civil matters, but it could not deal with cases involving real property, as these fell within the competence of

[28] Zaghlūl, pp. 194–195; Khānki, p. 4.

[29] Orders 504 and 518, as quoted in Zaghlūl, pp. 196–198.

the *sharī'ah* courts. The laws applied by this commission were generally those applied in the Ottoman Empire, and its judgments were appealable to Majlis al-Aḥkām.[30]

With the restoration of Majlis al-Aḥkām, it was natural also to restore the provincial councils with which it had been closely associated and to infuse them with a new life, especially since the populace was clamoring for such a step. Ismā'īl Pasha proceeded to do this upon assuming power in 1863. From 1870 to 1873 these councils were expanded and reorganized by several measures which resulted in the creation of four levels of jurisdiction below Majlis al-Aḥkām, ranging from courts of summary jurisdiction and petty claims in practically every town or small administrative unit, to courts of first instance in eight important centers (those of Cairo and Alexandria replaced the commercial councils there), and then to courts of appeal in Cairo, Ṭanṭa, and Asyūṭ, with Majlis al-Aḥkām the highest court of appeal.[31] The *sharī'ah* courts continued in theory to be the courts of general jurisdiction. In practice, however, their jurisdiction was gradually being limited to cases of personal status and those involving land. They had criminal jurisdiction over cases involving payment of blood money as a result of homicide, but the execution of such judgments was subject to approval by Majlis al-Aḥkām.

A further reorganization of the courts, along the lines later adopted by the national courts, was attempted in 1881, but the rebellion of the army elements under 'Arābi and the consequent British intervention defeated this attempt.

THE DEVELOPMENT OF THE LEGAL CODES

The military nature of Muḥammad 'Ali's rule in Egypt left its imprint upon the legal system he and his successors established. During the period before Ismā'īl Pasha there was a striking lack of attention to matters of civil law in the narrow sense. Laws

[30] Zaghlūl, pp. 199–200; Khānki, p. 6.
[31] Khānki, pp. 8–10.

and regulations enacted by the government dealt mostly with the punishment of criminals and matters of a public nature, such as the building of roads, bridges, canals, and factories. The pivot of the whole system was the establishment of governmental authority, the collection of taxes, and the amassing of wealth. Bribery of governmental officials and embezzlement were punished, not because they were wrong in themselves or because they hurt the interests of citizens, but because they reduced the income of government.[32] The military nature of the rule was also apparent in the composition of the judicial councils. Jam'iyyat al-Ḥaqqāniyyah was composed entirely of officers; even the Egyptian members of the Cairo Commission had to be officers.[33]

Under these circumstances it was quite natural that the judiciary was completely at the mercy of the administration. Sa'īd Pasha had twice abolished Majlis al-Aḥkām on sheer whim. The decisions of the high tribunals were dependent upon the executive order of the Khedive or the ketkhuda for enforcement. In the provinces the *mudīrs*, or administrative officers, were wont to use the members of the provincial judicial councils to carry out such purely administrative functions as the supervision of dikes along the Nile during the flood periods and the collection of taxes.[34] With this background even the establishment of the national courts did little to alter the *mudīr's* concept of himself as master of the judges who served in his province.[35]

Despite these unwholesome characteristics, which certainly

[32] See Zaghlūl, p. 239, and the authorities cited there.

[33] Khānki, p. 15.

[34] Zaghlūl, p. 243, relates that his brother, Shinnāwi Zaghlūl, president of a provincial judicial council of summary jurisdiction in 1875–1876 (1292 A.H.), was called upon by the *mudīr* of Gharbiyyah province, whose anger had been aroused by the district officer of Dasūq, to proceed to the house of the district officer, seize him, and confiscate all his effects. The *mudīr* evidently had sufficient power that the president of the judicial council was obligated to carry out these orders.

[35] See Zaghlūl, pp. 243–245, for a discussion of his experiences as a judge with the *mudīr* in Asyut in 1889.

were not typical of Western Europe in the nineteenth century, there was a conscious effort to imitate Europe in the legal as well as in the military and economic fields.[36] When al-Shūra al-Khuṣūṣiyyah was instituted in 1837 by Muḥammad ʻAli its composition was to be "in accordance with the practice current in Europe," and five years later, when Jamʻiyyat al-Ḥaqqāniyyah was instructed to look into the punishments meted out to state servants, it was to make an inquiry "about the practices current in Europe in this field." The European example was followed in codification as well. The preamble of the Siyāsat Nāmeh commented that "the various kingdoms in Europe possess various laws which agree with the nature, character and status of their people;"[37] hence the large body of laws and regulations issued by Muḥammad ʻAli and touching every phase of administration, from the regulation of government bureaus to control of the calling of donkey drivers in the market place. The two other codes in force in the country, the Ottoman Penal Code of 1851, adapted to Egyptian circumstances and applied only after the accession of Saʻīd Pasha in 1854,[38] and the Ottoman Commercial Code were either European inspired or of European origin. Only in purely civil matters did judges have recourse to Islamic law or to their own interpretations.

The feverish activity in judicial organization and legislation had created an atmosphere in which the public for the first time became acquainted with its rights and duties and the ways and means of their enforcement. In 1881, when the government proposed to reorganize the courts and issue new codes along the lines adopted three years later, the Egyptian government gazette *al-Waqāʼiʻ al-Miṣriyyah* declared jubilantly:[39]

[36] See Jamāl al-Dīn al-Shayyāl, *Tārīkh al-Tarjamah wa-al-Ḥarakah al-Thaqāfiyyah fi ʻAṣr Muḥammad ʻAli*, Cairo, 1951; Ibrahim Abu-Lughod, *Arab Rediscovery of Europe*, Princeton, N.J., 1963.

[37] Zaghlūl, p. 172.

[38] For the controversy between ʻAbbās Pasha and the Ottoman government concerning the application of this code in Egypt see Baer, pp. 32–38.

[39] *Al-Waqāʼiʻ al-Miṣriyyah*, no. 1003, January 4, 1881, as quoted in Zaghlūl, p. 218.

> The good tidings of reform have reached us, for an official source has intimated to us that the laws for the reform of the provincial [judicial] councils are almost ready . . . There is no doubt that this is one of the greatest reforms undertaken by the present government because the disequilibrium, generality, vagueness and deficiency of laws lead to loss of rights . . . and confusion. When rights and procedures are ascertained and everyone knows the precriptions of law, actions will become upright and confusion will diminish.

This activity in judicial organization and legislation was paralleled by intellectual activity in the field of law. In 1828 Muḥammad ʻAli sent the first student mission to Paris to study law. These students returned to Egypt in 1831 after having studied "natural law, international law, public law, political economy, statistics, and administration," and began to translate the collections of French laws and some legal textbooks.[40] This activity was centered in a school established in 1836, called Madrasat al-Alsun (School of Languages), under the direction of the Azharite *shaykh* Rifāʻah Rāfiʻ al-Ṭahṭāwi.[41] Ṭahṭāwi participated with some of his students in translating the French civil code into Arabic. He himself did a translation of the French commercial code that was published in 1868. His student Ṣāliḥ Majdi translated the code of preliminary inquiry (*Code d'instruction criminelle*), and two other students, ʻAbd Allāh Abu-al-Suʻūd and Ḥasan Fahmi, translated the code of civil procedure.[42]

A later student of this school, Muḥammad Qadri (1821 to 1888), gained renown as the foremost legal scholar of his age.

[40] M. K. Mursi, Kulliyyat al-Ḥuqūq, *al-Kitāb al-Dhahabi lil-Maḥākim al-Ahliyyah,* vol. I, Cairo, 1937, p. 410.

[41] For his biography see Jamāl al-Dīn Muḥammad al-Shayyāl, *Rifāʻah al-Ṭahṭāwi,* Cairo, 1945. An account of the School of Languages is found in J. Heyworth-Dunne, *An Introduction to the History of Education in Modern Egypt,* London, 1938, pp. 264–271.

[42] ʻAbd al-Raḥmān al-Rāfiʻi, *ʻAṣr Muḥammad ʻAli,* Cairo, 1947, pp. 401, 412–413.

In addition to his many early books on Arabic and French grammar and on geography, Qadri translated the French criminal code as a supplement to the other translations from the French. Although he had not studied at al-Azhar, but came instead from a secular background, he had a special fondness for Islamic law. After participating, with a committee created by the Ministry of Justice, in translating the codes of the recently established mixed courts from French into Arabic as a preparation for new codes for the proposed national courts, Qadri busied himself with a comparative study of French and Muslim law in the belief that the new codes must, in the last analysis, rest on a compromise between the two systems of laws. This study is still preserved in manuscript form at the Egyptian National Library in Cairo.[43]

As Minister of Justice during the rule of Tawfīq Pasha (1879 to 1892), Qadri was responsible for the work on the new codes and participated in formulating the Egyptian Civil Code, the Code of Preliminary Enquiry, and the Commercial Code. The works which brought him enduring fame were his three books codifying the rules of three fields of Muslim law: *Murshid al-Ḥayrān* for civil law or transactions, *al-Aḥkām al-Shar'iyyah* for personal status, and *Qānūn al-'Adl wa-al-Inṣāf* for *waqfs* or religious endowments. The first was apparently prepared at the behest of the government, which at first thought of basing the civil law of the country entirely on Muslim law but later changed its mind.[44] The other two have been considered basic works in their fields, not only in Egypt, but in several countries which apply the Ḥanafite rite.[45] Qadri's achievement has been compared with that of Napoleon in codifying the French civil code.[46]

[43] The study is entitled *Taṭbīq mā wujid fi al-Qānūn al-Madani muwāfiq li-madhhab abi-Ḥanīfah.*

[44] See the memorandum of Ḥusayn Fakhri Pasha, the Minister of Justice, dated December 7, 1882, as reproduced in *al-Kitāb al-Dhahabi lil-Maḥākim al-Ahliyyah,* vol. I, Cairo, 1937, p. 112.

[45] The personal-status code was translated into English by Wasey Sterry and N. Abcarius (London, 1914).

[46] For a complete biography of Qadri see Muḥammad Ḥusayn Haykal, *Tarājim Miṣriyyah wa-Gharbiyyah,* Cairo, n.d.

Madrasat al-Alsun later experienced a fluctuating existence. During the rule of ʻAbbās Pasha, from 1849 to 1854, it was closed down; it was reestablished under the name Madrasat al-Idārah wa-al-Alsun (School of Administration and Languages) by Ismāʻīl Pasha in 1868, under the direction of Victor Vidal, a French lawyer-engineer who had originally been called to Egypt to train Egyptian students in engineering. In 1882 it was split into two schools, one for administration and the other for languages. The school of administration was renamed Madrasat al-Ḥuqūq (School of Law) in 1886, but its primary function continued to be the training of officials for the various departments of the government. It is this school that became the School of Law of the Egyptian University (now Cairo University) when the university was founded in 1925.[47]

THE EARLY LEGAL PROFESSION

What of the legal profession, those whose business it was to represent clients before the courts? The *sharīʻah* courts had for a long time been the stamping ground of such a group, called *wukalāʼ* (attorneys), who loitered in the doorways of the courts waiting to accost potential clients. Their unscrupulousness gained them the epithet *muzawwirūn,* or forgers, and pious Muslim writers often inveighed against them.[48] During the rule of Muḥammad ʻAli a prominent official visitor to the *sharīʻah* court complained about the *wukalāʼ* whose "forgeries cannot be imagined to take place even in the countries of infidels" and who "picture the right to be wrong and the wrong right." Muḥammad ʻAli took the matter seriously and ordered that Dīwān al-Wāli investigate the matter. A list of fifteen *wukalāʼ* was drawn up, including the head of the North African loggia at al-Azhar and the head of the Ḥanafi *fatwa* (legal-opinion) office. The latter two were removed from office, and the others were banished from Cairo.[49] A further measure designed to curb their activity

[47] M. K. Mursi, pp. 410, 426.

[48] See Tyan, vol. I, pp. 400–404.

[49] For this case and subsequent developments pertaining to it see Zaghlūl, pp. 249–266.

was introduced in 1833, when Muḥammad ʿAli issued an order to the *qāḍi* of Cairo directing that court fees henceforth be collected from the *wukalā'*, who often brought baseless actions, rather than from the defendants, who, according to the rules of Muslim law, had been paying the fees even when they were judged innocent of any claim.[50]

A group akin to the *wukalā'*, and sometimes indistinguishable from them, were the *'arḍḥāljis,* or writers of complaints and statements of claim, whose number increased with the increase in judicial councils throughout the country. They originally practiced their humble calling, as indeed some still do, in front of courts and other governmental buildings, but when representation was allowed before the councils of merchants in Alexandria and Cairo their preparation of legal briefs became a recognized part of the judicial process and soon spread to other judicial councils.[51] These early advocates were innocent of any legal education or training, and their pleadings often consisted of a strange mixture of legal points and mendacious assertions. Any person who was adept at intercession with the judges and knew the ways and means of persuading government officials of his views was a successful advocate.[52]

[50] Zaghlūl, p. 268.

[51] Zaghlūl, pp. 268–270.

[52] Zaghlūl, pp. 281–283, relates on the authority of Shaykh Muḥammad ʿAbduh, the famous Egyptian Muslim reformer, the following story: A man named ʿAli ʿAsr, from the province of Buḥayrah, grew up as a peasant on the land. One day his brother-in-law was called as a witness in a preliminary inquiry of a crime in the province of Manūfiyyah. It was near dark when the witness arrived, so the *mudīr* ordered that he be held for the night in the local jail. The *mudīr* forgot all about him, and the poor wretch languished in jail for over two years without anybody knowing why he was there. When the government moved the prisoners to the Sudan, a large group of them, including the witness, were lodged in a Cairo fort on the way. This measure aroused ʿAli ʿAsr, who went to Cairo to see what could be done to free his brother-in-law. He lodged there with a fellow Buḥayran, Muḥammad ʿAbduh, who was then a student at al-Azhar. ʿAbduh tried to help him by drafting a petition to the

The period of Muḥammad ʻAli and his successors was thus one of experimentation in judicial organization, of rough-and-ready justice on the part of administrative officers, of abject submission by the judicial tribunals to the will of the Pasha or his administrative officials, but also of the inception of modern legal thinking and education, of codification of laws, and of a widespread legal knowledge among the people. The establishment of a rule of law and an efficient and just legal system, supported by a growing body of judges and lawyers aware of their role in the development of society, had to await the formation of the mixed courts and the national courts.

Ministry of the Interior explaining the sad lot of the prisoner and requesting his release. When the petition was ignored by the chief clerk, ʻAbduh advised his friend to accost the carriage of the minister on the way to his offices and to give him the petition personally. The minister, satisfied of the truth of the petition, ordered the release of the prisoner. ʻAsr took his brother-in-law back to their village, where they were met by a jubilant crowd which sang the glory of "ʻAli ʻAsr who brought back the prisoner." His fellow villagers, believing he was an able advocate, started to entrust their legal affairs to him, and his reputation skyrocketed. He then moved to Cairo, where he practiced his "profession" and became very rich.

CHAPTER TWO

the growth of a modern legal system

THE MIXED COURTS AND THE MIXED BAR ASSOCIATION

If any one factor were to be singled out as contributing the most to the modernization of Egypt, it would be the establishment in 1876 of the mixed courts, which represented a completely new solution to a chaotic situation. The councils of merchants in Cairo and Alexandria, established in 1845 and 1846, and the Cairo Commission, established in 1861, were the forerunners of this development in that their jurisdiction was over both foreign and Egyptian litigants. It was Nubar Pasha, however, who achieved this next difficult step. The chaos in the judicial field had not been limited to the Egyptian courts;

it also embraced the seventeen consular jurisdictions which were functioning under the mantle of treaties of capitulations and had assumed a great deal of power, since the commercial life of the country was almost exclusively in the hands of foreigners.

Nubar's achievement[1] in establishing the mixed courts was summarized in 1930 by J. Y. Brinton, the foremost authority on the subject:[2]

> The Mixed Courts of Egypt are the dominating judicial institution of the country. They correspond broadly to the federal judicial system in the United States. All litigation which involves a foreign interest (except suits between persons of the same nationality . . .), comes before them. As the activities of the one hundred and fifty thousand foreigners in Egypt largely control the commercial life of the fourteen million inhabitants, there is practically no litigation of any large or general importance which is not attracted to their jurisdiction. With a personnel of seventy judges (two-thirds of whom are foreigners selected from the principal countries of the world) and fourteen hundred employees, the courts have an annual output of some forty thousand written opinions. . . . No law can be passed affecting foreigners without the approval of the Mixed Courts. . . . They guarantee to foreigners as complete a protection of legal rights as exists in any country in the world. The Egyptian government is subject to their jurisdiction and their judgements. On the one hand, they are part of the judicial system of the Egyptian state; on the other, they are under the protection of a dozen foreign nations.

The mixed courts essentially comprised a court of appeals, which sat at Alexandria, and three district courts, at Cairo,

[1] Nubar himself often said, "Give Egypt water and justice and the country will become happy and prosperous." Quoted in 'Azīz Khānki, *al-Maḥākim al-Mukhtaliṭah*, Cairo, 1939, p. 62.

[2] J. Y. Brinton, *The Mixed Courts of Egypt*, New Haven, Conn., 1930, pp. xxiii–xxiv.

Alexandria, and Manṣūrah. Summary, police, and referee jurisdictions were also provided for. In ordinary civil and commercial cases the jurisdiction of the mixed courts covered all suits between Egyptians and foreigners and between foreigners of different nationality, with the exception of matters involving personal status, which were left to other tribunals. In criminal matters these courts had a considerable measure of—but not full—jurisdiction over foreigners. All the negotiations that led to the establishment of the mixed courts, the difficulties which beset the course of these negotiations, and the jurisdiction, procedure, and composition of these courts are ably presented in English by Brinton. Our concern here is with the manner in which these courts influenced the legal tradition of Egypt and prepared the way for the emergence of the national courts and modern lawyers.

The first advantage of the new system was the unification of jurisdiction, with the result that for the first time litigants had some idea of the court which might have to adjudicate the issue between them and the laws and procedures applicable. Previously, whenever a possibility of litigation had arisen, each foreign party had hastened to get his hands on the property that was the subject of litigation so that the suit would be brought before his own consul. If the defendants were of different nationalities, suit had to be brought in as many forums as there were defendants. In addition, appeals from consular decisions were generally heard in the home countries of the consuls.[3] The uniformity of jurisdiction brought about by the mixed courts contributed materially to the idea of a rule of law applicable to everybody. Nubar Pasha's original proposals had also been intended to protect the Egyptian government against raids upon the treasury by unscrupulous adventurers supported by their diplomatic representatives, and further, to protect the Egyptian people against the despotism of their rulers by a complete separation between the executive and judicial branches.[4] Although the mixed courts fulfilled the first purpose, their juris-

[3] Brinton, p. 9.
[4] Brinton, p. 27.

diction was not made large enough to include strictly "native" issues. However, the principle of separation of powers was established, and Nubar wasted no time in impressing its sanctity upon the judges of the national courts when the latter were set up.[5]

Another question intimately related to the rule of law was the standing and prestige of judges. In a country where judges had been the lackeys of the executive power or its agents, the foreign powers provided sufficient first-rank European jurists, at salaries far exceeding those of judges on the continent, to enable them to command respect. Their tenure was for life, and although they were officially appointed by the Khedive of Egypt, their discipline and impeachment, which was entrusted to their own court of appeal, rested in their own hands. The judges of the mixed courts were thus "to a singular degree . . . the undisturbed masters of their fate; the conditions of their existence minister to a degree of independence as complete as may be conceived in a judicial institution."[6]

Cases concerning the Khedive of Egypt and his estates provided further opportunity for the courts to stress the rule of law. When Khedive Ismā'īl failed to satisfy judgments against his estates, the courts threatened to withhold judgment in cases where the Egyptian government was a plaintiff. Later, when Germany protested to the Ottoman government that Ismā'īl's failure to satisfy judgments against his estate was a "direct violation of the international obligations" which had created the mixed courts and specified their jurisdiction, the Ottoman government, which held suzerainty over Egypt, sent him a telegram in which he was addressed as the "Ex-Khedive of Egypt."[7]

The codification of the laws themselves was a vital contribution to the establishment of a rule of law. Muḥammad 'Ali and his successors had issued a variety of laws, but most of these

[5] See Nubar's speech to the judges of the national courts, quoted in Khānki, pp. 63–64.

[6] Brinton, p. 89. See also on these points pp. 45, 86.

[7] Brinton, p. 48.

concerned administrative matters. The civil and commercial laws were not codified at all until the formation of the mixed courts. One might think that this difficult task would have been undertaken by a commission of jurists, but actually a Mr. Manoury, who was the secretary of the International Commission convened to examine the various projects of reform, carried it out singlehanded. He was apparently an expert lawyer thoroughly familiar with the special circumstances prevailing in Egypt, for his work, despite some justifiable criticisms, withstood the test of time and formed the basis for the codes of the national courts, established a few years later.[8] It was natural for him to base the codes upon French models, since the French language had dominated the intellectual life of Egypt and French legal norms were familiar to the commercial community. The civil code of the mixed courts differed from the French code, however, in that it excluded matters of personal status and included certain provisions of Muslim law, principally the institution of *shufʿah,* or preemption.

In this new legal atmosphere all factors pointed toward the emergence of a new class of able lawyers. The high educational standards of the new judges from Europe required that the professional pleaders before them have a similar legal education if the two parties were to speak a common language. Moreover, the ethical standards set by the new judges put at a premium the lawyer who knew his law and was able to persuade by legal argument, rather than the *wakīl* of bygone days, who had mastered the science of intercession and influence peddling. However, most of the litigation transferred to the mixed courts from the consular courts and the commercial councils of Cairo and Alexandria had been entrusted to *wukalāʾ*[9] or *mandataires* who were often without any legal education. When the mixed courts organized a bar association, it was found that these *mandataires* formed a large proportion of persons seeking admission. The bar decided at first to admit them to plead before the

[8] Brinton, pp. 145–147.
[9] Brinton, p. 24.

district courts and to restrict the pleading before the court of appeal to those with legal education. Then, ten years later, *mandataires* were restricted to the summary courts, and in time they were eliminated altogether.[10]

Although in the beginning there was no requirement of apprenticeship for admission to the mixed bar association, the raising of the level of lawyers necessitated such a step. Thus a regulation of June 9, 1887, introduced the French system of *stage,* whereby the *stagiaire* was required to go through a five-year apprenticeship before being allowed to plead before the district courts and a further period of three years of practice before pleading before the Court of Appeal.[11] At the end of the *stage* period a stiff practical and theoretical examination conducted by the bar's admission commission in a formal atmosphere of high dignity and decorum impressed upon the candidates and the general public the seriousness and high purpose of the profession.

The Mixed Bar Association started as an exclusively European organization; its membership consisted of European lawyers and *mandataires.* The Egyptian *wukalā'* who had practiced before the provincial councils did not figure among the early membership, perhaps because of their ignorance of foreign languages. At the first meeting of this bar, held on March 20, 1876, a George Mathier was elected president. In the next election, on November 15, 1877, not only were the officers elected entirely European, but not a single Arabic name figured among the seventy-nine members present.[12] A few years later Syrian names came into evidence, and gradually Egyptian subjects started to qualify for membership, until in 1930 they formed

[10] Brinton, p. 253. See also Raymond Schemeil, *De la profession d'avocat près les jurisdictions mixtes d'Égypte,* Alexandria, 1936, pp. 8–9.

[11] This requirement was found excessive, and five years later it was reduced to three years of apprenticeship and two years of practice. Brinton, p. 254; Schemeil, p. 10.

[12] Documents 1 and 2 of the register of the Mixed Courts, preserved in the offices of the National Bar Association, Cairo.

approximately half the membership, although only a small proportion were actually of Egyptian origin.[13]

Since the Mixed Bar was the forerunner of the National Bar Association, and was later merged with it, let us look briefly at its salient features. The first was the bar's close organization, reminiscent of the French bar or even of the guild system. Accordingly, the bar occupied an unusually prominent place in the life of the lawyer. The sense of pride in membership, the responsibility felt by the entire membership for the conduct of each member, and the assertion of the bar's prerogatives *vis-à-vis* the courts and the general public all served to heighten the feeling of close association. Another feature, stemming from the first, was the creation in 1928 of a mutual-benefit fund which drew its capital from dues, voluntary subscriptions, and special gifts and legacies. Such funds had already proved their worth in some continental countries, including France, Belgium, and Greece. The purpose of the fund was to advance interest-free loans to members and to pay annual pensions to those qualifying. A third feature was that lawyers were prohibited from engaging in other pursuits lest they compromise the dignity of the profession or their attention to the profession be lessened. It is interesting to note that the proprietorship and even editorship of a newspaper were not considered incompatible with the legal profession—a decision which certainly encouraged the close future association of the legal profession and journalism.[14]

THE NATIONAL COURTS AND MODERN LAWYERS

The influence of the mixed courts in spreading the rule of law was not so widely felt at the popular level because the mixed courts were concerned mainly with European interests. During

[13] Brinton, p. 257. The diversity of the nationalities of members may be gauged from the *Report of the Judicial Adviser for the Year* 1916: Egyptian or Ottoman 191, Greek 11, Italian 75, French 62, British 24, Austro-Hungarian 18, other nationalities 25.

[14] For a detailed treatment of some of these points see Brinton, pp. 258–265.

the sittings of the International Commission of Judicial Reforms in 1881, M. Giaccone, the second Italian delegate and vice-president of the court of appeal at Alexandria, proposed that the jurisdiction of the mixed courts be extended to cases between native Egyptians on the application of the litigants. However, the Egyptian government considered this proposal "subversive of the authority of the Khedive and of the independence of the country." The British delegate, Sir E. Malet, also opposed the proposal; in a dispatch on July 20, 1881, to Earl Granville, the Foreign Secretary, he said: "Any extension of the jurisdiction of the Mixed Courts to natives must largely increase the influence of the courts. This influence is thoroughly international, and therefore prejudicial to the aim which I have been instructed constantly to bear in mind, of keeping out of Egypt, at all hazards, the interference of countries other than England and France in the administration." A memorandum accompanying the dispatch gave additional grounds for the opposition: ". . . The true remedy for arbitrary acts of government is the existence of indigenous courts administering laws in harmony with the degree of development which a country is aiming at within its practical reach."[15]

Actually, during the previous year the Egyptian government had been preparing a scheme for such a system of indigenous courts, and Malet had "the satisfaction to inform" his chief in London that the charter for the new "native" system of justice had been finally considered and sanctioned on October 29, 1881, and that the decree establishing the courts had been issued on November 17, 1881.[16] The events of the 'Arābi movement, however, delayed this important reform for another two years.

Following the British bombardment of Alexandria on July 11, 1882, and the subsequent British occupation of Egypt, the issue of the national courts again came up for consideration. Ḥusayn Fakhri Pasha, the Minister of Justice, submitted on December 7, 1882, a memorandum on the subject to the Council

[15] Foreign Office Document 78/3376, sec. 19.

[16] Foreign Office Document 78/3376, secs. 33, 37.

of Ministers. After reviewing the status of the existing courts and the laws they applied, the memorandum stated:[17]

> It is clear . . . that the [present courts] are of three levels, that all but summary cases are not disposed of until they are examined at these three levels, that no sufficient laws exist, that the administrative powers are mixed up with the judicial powers, that most cases remain pending—because of the above-mentioned reasons—for years, and that judgments which do issue are dependent upon the opinions and interpretations of judges. All these matters require reform.

The memorandum went on to say that two things were needed, adequate laws suited to the customs of the people and judges who were both independent and able to fill the new positions. It is significant that with regard to laws the memorandum dismissed the efforts of the previous government to have Muḥammad Qadri Pasha codify a civil law based on the *sharī'ah*

[17] The full text of the memorandum is reproduced in *al-Kitāb al-Dhahabi lil-Maḥākim al-Ahliyyah*, vol. I, Cairo, 1937, pp. 107–115. The state of criminal justice specifically was the subject of another report (Foreign Office Document 78/3454) dated December 5, 1882, by Major Herbert Chermside of the British Agency in Cairo. This report, written in the aftermath of the 'Arābi revolt, speaks of the "universal complaints on the part of so-called political prisoners, of prisoners charged with riots, and of ordinary prisoners, as to the long time they have been incarcerated without either examination or trial." Appendix A of the report attempts to point out the reason for this sad state: "There seems no hard and fast line between executive and judicial, the powers of the former varying according to the presence or absence of a court in any locality. The executive generally exercises the functions of *juge d'instruction,* and the courts appear usually to pronounce sentence on the documentary evidence, without summoning the accused. . . . Unjust detention in prison without examination becomes possible and frequent. . . . When it is considered that at many places there are many prisons where the executive can confine, but no courts, the injustice liable to occur in the absence of fixed terms of assize for cases is obvious."

with the comment that this codification was not yet complete.[18] It further questioned whether such a law would be in harmony with the customs and transactions of the people, either Egyptian or foreign. Instead it recommended the adoption of the laws then being applied in the mixed courts, with some modifications to be introduced by a special commission.[19] On the second issue the memorandum recommended the selection of judges from among the Egyptian members of the mixed courts, the "effendis" who had studied law in Europe, the European residents in Egypt who were acquainted with the laws, language, and customs of the people, with some of the foreign judges of the mixed courts who had acquired a thorough knowledge of the nature and customs of the people to be appointed in the higher ranks. As justification for the inclusion of foreigners in a national-courts scheme, Fakhri stated that the mixed courts were an exceptional arrangement which would not have existed had the Europeans had faith in the Egyptian courts, and that the inclusion of foreign judges, if it did not bring about the demise of the mixed courts in a short time, should at least be conducive to the reference of mixed-court cases in distant areas to the new national courts.[20]

On the question of jurisdiction of the national versus the *sharīʿah* courts the memorandum had this to say:[21]

> Another question which merits attention is the existence of *sharīʿah* courts side by side with the civil [national] courts. The former have the competence to deal with all cases submitted to them, whether they pertain to personal status, civil law, or criminal law. If this were to continue—keeping in mind the differences in the laws and procedures of the two systems—a great harm would result . . . for if a person

[18] On Qadri Pasha's codification achievements see the discussion in Chapter 1.

[19] *Al-Kitāb al-Dhahabi*, p. 112.

[20] *Al-Kitāb al-Dhahabi*, p. 115.

[21] *Al-Kitāb al-Dhahabi*, p. 113.

were entirely free to submit his case to the court he desired, then both systems would lose their respect and influence. . . . Accordingly, it is necessary to define the competence of both systems: to limit the jurisdiction of *sharī'ah* courts to personal status and to make the other cases, be they civil, commercial, or criminal within the jurisdiction of the civil courts.

When the memorandum was examined by the Council of Ministers on December 21. 1882, it was adopted with practically no change. The discussion revealed that the other ministers were even more sanguine than Fakhri in anticipating the early demise of the mixed courts if European judges were to be appointed in the native courts.[22] It was agreed, therefore, to appoint one foreign judge to each court of first instance and two foreign judges to each court of appeal.[23] It was further agreed that Majlis al-Aḥkām, which, as the highest court of appeal, was also called Maḥkamat al-Tamyīz, or Court of Cassation, be done away with, making the national courts correspond to the mixed courts in having only two levels.[24] The discussion revealed that there were at least three ministers who disliked limiting the jurisdiction of the *sharī'ah* courts, but the recommendations of the memorandum on the point were adopted.[25]

On December 30, 1883, the various judicial appointments were made. As eventually constituted—that is, when Upper Egypt was later brought under their sway—the new national courts comprised a comprehensive system of summary, district, and criminal courts covering the entire territory of Egypt. At first only one court of appeal, with a chamber of cassation for criminal cases, was created in Cairo, but in 1925 another court

[22] Sharīf Pasha expected the demise in three or four months. See the account of part of the discussion reproduced in Khānki, pp. 189–191.

[23] The number of foreign judges was later reduced gradually, until only one was left in 1930.

[24] A court of cassation was reinstated, however, on May 2, 1931.

[25] Khānki, p. 191.

of appeal was established in Asyūṭ. The British Judicial Adviser to the Egyptian government reported in 1896 that between twenty and thirty European judges, mostly from Holland and Belgium, had arrived in the country, but that almost all of them had returned home because of "the difficulty of assimilating [themselves] to the life, ways, and climate of the East." He seemed glad, though, that four new British judges had remained who knew Arabic and were young enough to accommodate themselves to the ways and conditions of an Eastern country.[26] To uphold the prestige of the national courts the Egyptian government maintained the salary of their judges at a figure slightly higher than that of the judges of the mixed courts, a measure which tended to draw Egyptian judges from the mixed courts.[27]

With regard to the law to be applied in the new courts, the Council of Ministers approved Fakhri's recommendations and decreed that the laws applicable in the mixed courts be followed, with the exception of the penal code and the code of preliminary enquiry, which were to be amended for conformity to the conditions in the country.[28] However, separate codes were prepared. An Italian lawyer named Moriondo prepared the civil code, in collaboration with Muḥammad Qadri Pasha. Another Italian, Fāscir (?), prepared the penal code, the preliminary-enquiry code, and the commercial code, the latter two in collaboration with Qadri Pasha. Buṭrus Ghāli Pasha, who was then Undersecretary of the Ministry of Justice, also participated in the preparation of these codes. Questions which touched upon Islamic law were referred for comment to Shaykh Baḥrāwi, Mufti of the Ministry of Justice.[29] It is interestng to note that all codes were first prepared in French and then translated into Arabic.

[26] Memorandum of Sir J. Scott appended to the *Annual Report* of Sir E. Baring (later Lord Cromer), 1896, p. 27.

[27] Brinton, p. 279.

[28] *Al-Kitāb al-Dhahabi,* p. 115.

[29] Khānki, p. 92.

The national courts, or native courts, as they were called by the British,[30] started functioning in March, 1884. From the beginning they seemed to have a salutary influence on the development of a rule of law throughout the country. Baring (later Lord Cromer), in his report for 1891 on the finances and general condition of Egypt, admitted the shortcomings of the new courts because of "a badly-directed choice of men at their foundation" but had this to say about them:[31]

> The new tribunals are a great advance on their predecessors. The work done had quadrupled in the last six years. There are few arrears. Decisions are not only taken but executed. . . . . I have not heard of any well-established charge of corruption. The New Courts exercise their powers with great caution. They demur about proof, they reject confessions, and rarely punish when there is any possibility of the innocence of the accused. Their anxiety to protect the innocent seems, without doubt, strange to the officials trained under the old regime, who used to seize men under slight suspicion, to take presumption of guilt as sufficient evidence, to force confessions by torture, and to inflict speedy punishments which were effectual in striking terror.

The Egyptian government, not so confident of the efficiency of the new courts in dealing with crime, had set up special commissions of brigandage with ruthless methods. After reviewing the work of these commissions and their eventual abolishment following his remonstrances, Baring stated that it had soon become apparent that in avoiding the evils of the commissions of brigandage a serious danger had arisen: the crime rate had doubled between 1885 and 1889.[32] The report went on to say:

> It had become abundantly clear that the Egyptian government was unable to deal with the very considerable

[30] For the campaign to get rid of the admittedly unflattering term "native" see Khānki, pp. 197–198.

[31] Foreign Office Document 78/4408, pp. 102–109.

[32] The "doubling" of the rate of crime might, of course, have been the result of a better system of reporting and recording crimes.

difficulties of the situation without European assistance. It was under these circumstances that . . . I moved the Egyptian government to appoint Mr. [later Sir John] Scott to the post of Judicial Adviser. This proposal encountered a certain amount of opposition, but it was warmly supported by His Highness the Khedive. Mr. Scott has, therefore, been appointed.

There was no mistaking the point that the establishment and strengthening of a rule of law was a difficult and painful process: "The main faults of the new Tribunals are those inherent in a new system, which is somewhat in advance of the civilization of the country and has not been subjected to steady and enlightened supervision." But once it was firmly seated, the system moved steadily forward. "The protecting power and its judicial advisers enabled the new judges in Egypt to safeguard rights and liberties; even *mudīrs* and *pāshās* who dared to violate the law were brought to trial. In fact, the men around the Khedive were not immune to the authority of the law. The Khedive and any one of his subjects became equal before the law."[33]

In this equalitarian atmosphere seething with the ideas of rights vindicated and liberties safeguarded it was natural that the legal profession flourished. Courts, judges, and judicial proceedings became not only topics of public interest, but instruments of public education. In an especially litigious country judges and lawyers assumed the role of great national figures.

As was the case with the first group of lawyers of the mixed courts, the lawyers of the national courts were drawn initially from the *wukalā'*, the only available source. This gave the legal profession in its early days an unsavory reputation. Ibrāhīm al-Hilbāwi, the first president of the National Bar Association, relates in his unpublished memoirs that in 1887, when he married one of the Circassian maids at the khedivial palace, the other maids were curious about his profession of *abukāto,* or advocate. Upon inquiring from the *bāsh agha* (chief officer)

[33] 'Abd al-Ḥalīm al-Jundi, *al-Hilbāwi,* Cairo, n.d., p. 21.

of the palace, they were told that an *abukāto* was a "forger and a swindler."[34] Even a decade later the legal profession was not completely acceptable in some conservative circles. When Muḥammad Farīd, the well-known Egyptian nationalist leader, opened a law office in 1897, his father, who was director of the khedivial estates, and who happened to be in Geneva at the time, was heard to complain to Shaykh Muḥammad 'Abduh, the famous reformer, "Is it right and proper, sir, that Muḥammad Farīd should disgrace me in my later years by opening an advocate's shop?"[35]

It was fortunate for the legal profession that the careers of some men who were to become among the most famous in Egypt started in connection with the law. Several students of the Muslim political thinker and activist Jamāl-al-Dīn al-Afghāni at al-Azhar University became either judges or lawyers. Muḥammad 'Abduh, who established his reputation as a social and religious reformer, was appointed a judge in 1888 and was promoted in 1895 to deputy counselor in the court of appeal, where he served in the latter office until he was appointed Mufti of Egypt in 1899.[36]

Sa'd Zaghlūl, the future leader of the Wafd Party, joined the ranks of the advocates in 1885, "unknown to his family and friends," who would have looked askance at such a venture. But he "was not made lowly by this profession as was feared; instead, he raised its status."[37] In 1892, at the suggestion of Muḥammad 'Abduh, he was appointed deputy judge at the court of appeal and became the first advocate to hold a judicial office. The importance of this step could not fail to make its mark upon lawyers and judges alike. It moved the vice-president of the court, at a party held by a group of lawyers honoring Zaghlul on the occa-

[34] Al-Jundi, pp. 22–23.

[35] Memoirs of Aḥmad Luṭfi al-Sayyid, *al-Muṣawwar,* September 7, 1950.

[36] *Al-Kitāb al-Dhahabi,* pp. 468, 471.

[37] 'Abbās Maḥmūd al-'Aqqād, *Sa'd Zaghlūl,* Cairo, 1936, pp. 71, 73.

sion of his appointment, to say, "This appointment is an indication that advocacy and the judiciary are two equal entities."[38] Advocacy had come into its own. Ibrāhīm al-Liqāni, a former colleague of Zaghlūl at al-Azhar University and in the legal profession, on the same occasion expressed the assurance of the new profession in words that later became one of the literary pieces to be memorized by school children. After congratulating Zaghlūl on his new position he said,[39]

> But why do we congratulate you?
> Have you been transferred to a position that would make you richer or more prosperous? Nay. . . . Have you been transferred to a position in which you would practice a knowledge you did not practice before? . . . Nay. Why, then, do we congratulate you? We do so because you used to defend the right, strive for equity and struggle for justice when the latter was not in your hands, while, now, justice is in your hands, and the right is sought from you.

Another student of al-Afghāni who became prominent in the field of law was Ibrāhīm al-Hilbāwi, who gained the enmity of the entire nation when he prosecuted the Egyptian peasants who had killed some British soldiers at Denshiway. Later, however, primarily because of his defense of nationalist and popular causes in the courts, he so ingratiated himself with the nation that he was elected president of the National Bar Association upon its formation in 1912.[40]

Zaghlūl, al-Hilbāwi, and al-Liqāni, along with Aḥmad al-Ḥusayni, were the most prominent lawyers in the mainstream of Egyptian life. They were all without any formal modern legal

[38] Al-'Aqqād, p. 79.

[39] Al-'Aqqād, pp. 79–80. Al-Liqāni, who, like Zaghlūl, became an advocate in 1885, had also been a student of al-Afghāni. He later became the lawyer for the estates of Ismā'īl's wives and seems to have been a leader in the profession. Interview with the late Dr. Sani al-Liqāni (his son) in February, 1958.

[40] For a sympathetic biography of al-Hilbāwi, see al-Jundi, *al-Hilbāwi.*

education,[41] but their training at al-Azhar and thorough grounding in Islamic law gave them an advantage over their foreign and Christian colleagues in winning great popularity. Actually, until 1888 there were only thirteen Muslim lawyers among the first forty-five registered with the Court of Appeal, so these four Azharites had little competition in popularity.[42] Zaghlūl and al-Hilbāwi, however, seem to have had the ability and independence of spirit that would have made them shine in any locale. Despite their astonishingly similar backgrounds, they were political rivals for almost half a century. Both supported the 'Arābi movement, as did most Azharites; in fact, Zaghlūl was later tried and acquitted of the charge of conspiring to kill the witnesses who had given testimony against the rebels. Both had been employed in 1880 as assistants to Muḥammad 'Abduh in editing *al-Waqā'i' al-Miṣriyyah,* the official gazette of the Egyptian government. It was in this capacity that they became acquainted with the various administrative and judicial functions of the state, and even absorbed considerable legal knowledge, for the gazette was empowered to publish and review some of the more important judgments of the old courts. Thus they brought to the legal profession abilities and experience not shared by many of their colleagues. Zaghlūl went on to the judiciary and then to a position of dominance in the political life of Egypt, while al-Hilbāwi continued to excel at law.[43]

The really able lawyers in these early days, however, were very few. The profession continued to be plagued by a host of practitioners who lacked the necessary legal knowledge and the ethical standards for a viable profession. Moreover, it lacked a law defining its membership, the duties and rights of members, and their relation to their clients and to the courts. The only

[41] Zaghlūl obtained his *license en droit* in 1897, after he was appointed judge.

[42] Interview with Abu-Sarī' 'Abd al-'Azīz, chief archivist of the National Bar Association, in March, 1962.

[43] Al-'Aqqād, pp. 63, 72; al-Jundi, pp. 18–19.

reference to the legal profession in the Courts Organization Law of June 14, 1883, was an article allowing representation in proceedings before the courts and another which empowered every court to deny a person the right to represent others if "he is not suitable or well equipped to undertake the duties of representation."[44] In other words, the whole question of legal representation was left entirely in the hands of the courts, and there was no provision for the rights and duties of advocates. The Rules of Court of February 14, 1884, merely regulated how a power of attorney given to an advocate was to be filed, stipulated that an advocate return documents to his client after the case was settled, and other such questions of detail.[45] A resolution of the court of appeal dated May 3, 1884, stipulated that a person wishing to represent others must produce a certificate of "uprightness and good conduct" authenticated by the Attorney General.[46] It was not until December 18, 1888, that the Egyptian government, desirous of putting an end to the chaos in the legal profession, issued an Advocates Law in an attempt to clarify this situation. The law set up a register of advocates in which the names of qualified lawyers were to be inscribed. To qualify, a candidate was required to have reached the age of twenty-one, to have enjoyed a good reputation, to be proficient in the art of advocacy, and not to have been subjected to a judgment or disciplinary action that compromised his honor. The "proficiency" in advocacy was not spelled out; this was left to the judgment of a special admission committee, which examined the candidate in whatever manner it saw fit.

Needless to say, there still was general dissatisfaction with the status of the profession. The examining committee seems to have been so lax in admitting candidates that many lawyers were so only in name. Besides, there were no specific prescrip-

[44] Articles 24 and 25, respectively.

[45] Articles 50 and 52, respectively, later repealed by Law 26 for the year 1912.

[46] Zaghlūl, pp. 303–304.

tions for legal education or knowledge of languages.[47] A new Advocates Law was issued on September 16, 1893, which stipulated that no person's name could be inscribed in the register of advocates unless, in addition to being of good character and a resident of Egypt, he had obtained a diploma from the Khedivial Law School or a diploma from a foreign law school, provided that the foreign diploma was considered by the admission committee to be equivalent to the Egyptian diploma.[48] A later amendment to this law made it, in effect, obligatory for a candidate with a foreign diploma to know Arabic and to pass an examination in subjects not taught abroad: Islamic law, Egyptian criminal law, laws of procedure, and Egyptian administrative law.[49] The same amendment also made it possible for a person who had served for a period of five years as a judge or as a member of the Attorney General's office to be admitted into the profession.

It is interesting to note that this law for the first time referred to lawyers as *avocatos,* or advocates, as well as designating them by the Arabic term *muḥāmūn.* The government, it seems, had considered the French term *avocat* or the Italian *avocato,* as representing a type of lawyer far superior to those practicing before the national courts, whom they called first *wukalā'* and later *muḥāmūn.* Zaghlūl relates that "the men of the mixed courts" considered the term *avocat* as reserved for themselves and objected to lawyers practicing before the national courts being likened to them.[50] However, since the new law demanded the same qualifications of the lawyers before the national courts that had been demanded of their colleagues before the mixed courts, there was no longer any reason for the distinction.

In addition to the provisions discussed above, the new law

[47] See Zaghlūl's memorandum on the subject in Zaghlūl, pp. 313–315.

[48] Article 2 of the Advocates Law.

[49] Amendment dated February 20, 1898.

[50] Zaghlūl, p. 317.

spelled out the rights and duties of advocates in reasonable detail and dealt with a host of questions pertaining to the profession, such as the secrecy of a client's business, the fees payable to an advocate, free legal aid to the poor, the incompatibility of the legal profession with pursuits that might tend to degrade it, the discipline of errant advocates by the court, and the wearing of a special black robe at judicial hearings.[51] The law was mainly concerned, however, with the requirement for legal diplomas. Many of the advocates who had been admitted to practice before some courts had no such diplomas, and their rights, it was found, were not equal to those of their colleagues, especially in the matter of being allowed to practice before other courts of comparable degree.[52] Consequently, on May 5, 1910, when Sa'd Zaghlūl was Minister of Justice, a law was passed granting to advocates who had no diplomas but had proved their ability through long years of practice, complete equality with those who had obtained diplomas.[53]

[51] The Advocates Law has been revised several times: in 1912, in 1939, in 1944, and in 1957.

[52] In this regard see the complaints of Emin Schemeil, the editor of *al-Ḥuqūq,* in vol. 8, September 23, 1893, pp. 241–243.

[53] Law 9 for the year 1910.

CHAPTER THREE

the development of the legal profession

THE NATIONAL BAR ASSOCIATION

The Advocates Law of September 16, 1893, went a long way toward giving the legal profession a recognition and defining the rights and duties of its members, but even before this law was issued there had been demands for a professional organization that would be represented in administering examinations to candidates and in disciplining members.[1] The law itself made no provision for advocates to share in these functions, which

[1] *Al-Ḥuqūq*, vol. 8, June 3, 1893, p. 107.

continued to be primarily the responsibility of the courts, nor did it set up an organization for them. At this time the legal profession had not attained sufficient maturity, sufficient number, or a degree of professional responsibility that would entitle them to these things. In fact, it took almost twenty years for this development to materialize.

In 1910, when Sa'd Zaghlūl was appointed Minister of Justice, 'Azīz Khānki, a prominent member of the profession, addressed an open letter to him requesting that a bar association be formed.[2] After stating that lawyers in France were about to hold the centennial celebration of the founding of the bar association there, Khānki went on to stress the necessity of such an organization for the proper discharge of a lawyer's duties. He maintained that the legal profession could not fulfill those duties without being truly independent, and that independence could not be attained without an organization to establish and safeguard it. He complained that in Egypt the position of lawyers *vis-à-vis* judges and members of the Attorney General's office was so weak that the right of defense was jeopardized, and that the lack of an organization empowered to settle differences among lawyers resulted in a host of civil, and even criminal, cases being raised by some lawyers against some others. Khānki's letter concluded with a request that the minister come to the aid of his "second family" (advocacy; the first being the judiciary) and create an organization for the profession.[3]

Early in 1912 a group of lawyers met in Cairo to discuss the formation of a bar association and sent a delegation to meet with Zaghlūl and elicit his support for the project. Zaghlūl promised to act and hastened to prepare a law that would realize their demand. The law (Law 26 for the year 1912) was issued on September 30, 1912—after Zaghlūl had been succeeded

[2] The letter published in *al-Jarīdah,* October 16, 1910, is reproduced in 'Azīz Khānki and Jamīl Khānki, *al-Muḥāmāh Qadīman wa-Ḥadīthan,* Cairo, 1939, pp. 15–19.

[3] Khānki, *al-Muḥāmāh,* pp. 17, 19.

in the Ministry of Justice by Ḥusayn Rushdi Pasha—and a meeting of the general assembly of the National Bar Association was set for November 1, 1912, to elect a board.[4] The explanatory memorandum attached to the law stated that the profession had come a long way since the days when its membership consisted of *wukalā'* who lacked legal qualifications and therefore had to be placed under the supervision of the judiciary. "Now," the memorandum continued, "most members have made a thorough study of law, and therefore it is to the interest of the profession to obtain some independence."

On November 1, 1912, at the invitation of Yaḥya Ibrāhīm Pasha, president of the court of appeal, 332 lawyers who practiced before the court of appeal and the courts of first instance met at the court of appeal building in Cairo to elect the members of the board and the president and vice-president of the new bar association. Of the fifteen lawyers elected, twelve had practiced for ten years or more and three had practiced for a lesser period. The law had weighted this membership to assure adequate representation for those with greater experience. Ibrāhīm al-Hilbāwi, who had gained prominence as an especially able lawyer, was elected first president of the National Bar Association, despite the fact that he had compromised himself as a prosecuting attorney in the Denshiway trials.[5] Owing to the role lawyers played in the public life of Egypt, the election of the president of the bar became an event of national importance, and the keen competition between individuals and parties often threatened violence—although, ironically, when there were no elections or questions of political importance, it was difficult to muster a quorum.

Financially the beginnings of the bar association were rather modest. The budget for the year 1913 was set at

[4] Khānki, *al-Muḥāmāh,* p. 20; 'Aziz Khānki, *al-Maḥākim al-Mukhtaliṭah wa-al-Maḥakīm al-Ahliyyah,* Cairo, 1939, pp. 176–177.

[5] *Minutes of the General Assembly of the National Bar Association,* part I, p. 284.

£E1,655, to be collected from the yearly fees,[6] from fees of admission to the bar, and from contributions. The bulk of the expenditure was to go for rent, for clerks and minor employees, and for the local bar committees to be set up in the provinces. The provision for buying books for the bar library was £E50.[7]

From the start the activities of the board were varied. It prepared the bar rules (internal law), which embraced such questions as *stage*, control of the lawyers' register, fees payable, aid to needy colleagues, and settlement of disputes among lawyers or between lawyers and clients. It also disposed of a large number of complaints by citizens against lawyers, several complaints by lawyers against other lawyers, and three cases between lawyers and members of the Attorney General's office. In addition, it made the necessary preparations for a suitable library and for future public lectures on legal topics.[8] As the years rolled by these activities increased in intensity and variety. The report of the board for the year 1915 mentioned a successful intercession with the Disciplinary Council to reconsider an action, of the actual establishment of a bar library, of several public lectures delivered in Ṭanṭa, Alexandria, and Cairo, and even of several legal opinions in response to questions by members.[9] In addition, the board had been empowered by the 1912 law to appoint two lawyers to the Admission Committee, which was also composed of the president and a counselor of the court of appeal and the Attorney General, and to have its president or a deputy sit on the Disciplinary Council, which also included the president and three counselors of the court of appeal.[10] The latter two provisions undoubtedly imparted to the bar a large

[6] The number of lawyers expected to pay fees were 280 practicing before the court of appeal, at £E3 each, 230 practicing before the courts of first instance, at £E2 each, and 120 undergoing a period of apprenticeship at £E1 each.

[7] *Minutes*, part I, p. 277.

[8] *Minutes*, part I, p. 271.

[9] *Minutes*, part I, pp. 259–256.

[10] Articles 3 and 26, respectively.

measure of prestige, gave the individual lawyer a feeling of being represented in matters which affected his professional interests, and consequently made him more independent in discharging his duties—an obvious contribution to the rule of law.

By 1916 the National Bar Association had made so much progress that the British Judicial Adviser foresaw the possibility of its fusion with the Mixed Bar. He even seemed to think that the National Bar had higher professional standards than the Mixed Bar and said that many young men had flocked to the Mixed Bar who did not possess the necessary qualifications for admission to the National Bar or, in the case of foreigners, to the bars of their own countries.[11]

To propagate legal principles and judgments which contained such principles and to publish laws and decrees and criticism of judgments and laws, the board decided to issue a journal, *al-Muḥāmāh.* This journal first appeared in 1920 and has been published continuously since then. The board also strove for adequate representation in the commissions set up by the Ministry of Justice for the revision of laws.[12] To encourage legal research among lawyers, it set up two prizes for the best treatises on civil- and criminal-law topics and other prizes for similar studies by students at the Law School.[13]

The welfare of its members and their families also engaged the early attention of the bar. In addition to some donations to needy colleagues, in 1925 the bar established a fund to help the families of deceased members, although payments into it lapsed, so that it was discontinued in 1927. Six years later, when the Ministry of Justice was contemplating the revision of the Advocates Law, the bar proposed the establishment of a provident fund for its members, but political developments delayed this step until the latter part of 1938, when the government contributed £E5,000 toward such a fund and then followed it

[11] *Report of the Judicial Adviser for the Year* 1916, pp. 30–31.
[12] *Minutes,* part I, p. 132.
[13] *Minutes,* part II, p. 708.

up in 1940 with a further sum of £E12,500. These sums, plus 50 percent of the proceeds from fees of admission, 40 percent of the yearly subscriptions, a special stamp tax, and yearly government contributions, were able to provide in 1940 a monthly maximum retirement pay of £E12 for each lawyer; the amount gradually increased to £E24 in 1950.[14] The commodity shortages and high prices during World War II prompted the bar in 1943 to establish a consumer cooperative for its members.[15]

The National Bar Association today occupies a handsome and spacious building next to the law courts on one of the more elegant streets in Cairo. The laying of its cornerstone on February 13, 1937, by King Farouk and other notables was a memorable occasion in Cairo.[16]

The bar membership, already large in 1949, was further swelled that year by the absorption of the membership of the Mixed Bar, as provided in a declaration issued on May 8, 1937, by the Egyptian delegation to the Montreux conference, which terminated foreign capitulations in Egypt, including the mixed courts.[17] In 1956 there was another great increase in the membership as a result of the abolishment of the *sharīʿah* courts and the absorption of the Sharīʿah Bar Association. In neither case was the provident fund affected, as the Mixed Bar and the Sharīʿah Bar had their own provident funds. By March, 1957, there were 6,391 regular members of the bar, 401 former members of the Mixed Bar, and 412 former members of the Sharīʿah

[14] *Minutes,* part II, pp. 630–629, 245. At this time the yearly government contribution was £E9,000. This sum was understood to be in lieu of the free legal aid given by the bar.

[15] *Minutes,* part II, p. 525.

[16] A description of the ceremony is found in *Minutes,* part II, pp. 733–729.

[17] Appendix to *al-Muḥāmāh,* vol. 17, no. 10, June, 1937, pp. 16–17, for the declaration; *Minutes,* part II, p. 314, for acceptance of the Mixed Bar members. Law 51 for the year 1949 empowered the National Bar to admit these members. The mixed courts, after a period of transition, came to an end on October 14, 1949.

Bar, making a total of 7,204 practicing lawyers. It is interesting to note that women lawyers numbered 157, but not all of them were practicing.[18]

The protection of the rights and privileges of lawyers occupied a sizable part of the board's time. In addition to disposition of the usual complaints by and against lawyers and members of the Attorney General's office or the public, the board took a variety of actions to ameliorate the lot of the lawyers or to preserve their dignity. Among such actions were the assessment of legal fees when such fees were in dispute; representations that in appointing lawyers to defend indigent defendants the courts refrain from selecting those who had to travel a long way to the scene of the trial, and representations that the courts inform defense lawyers beforehand whenever a scheduled trial could not be held at the appointed time so that lawyers should not waste valuable time in traveling.[19]

The really important intercession by the bar on behalf of its members involved both the judiciary and the Council of Ministers. It is in relation to these two entities that the bar strove to keep its independence and that of its members in the performance of their function. The quasi-balance thus created doubtless had its effect in strengthening the rule of law. The first recorded incident of conflict between lawyers and judges occurred in 1926, when lawyers in Manṣūrah went on strike for an indignity one of their members had suffered at the hands of the local court. The board interceded and stopped the strike pending the investigation of the incident. In the same year the Minister of Justice, following representations made by the board, reprimanded two provincial judges for insulting two lawyers pleading before them and insisted that "advocacy should have the utmost respect."[20] The real measuring of swords between the

[18] Interview with Yūsuf al-Masri, secretary of the National Bar Association, in February, 1958.

[19] These representations were made in 1921. See *Minutes,* part I, p. 213.

[20] *Minutes,* part I, p. 133.

bar and the judiciary took place some three years later, when lawyers pleading in three courts were fined £E50 each for contempt of court. No sooner had the first incident occurred, in Rosetta, than the president of the bar met with the authorities and requested suspension of the sentence. Then the board met in an extraordinary session and demanded that the Minister of Justice investigate the incident. Later the board delegated the president and another able lawyer to defend the convicted lawyer before the chamber of cassation and to insist that a lawyer could not be fined while pleading in court. The defense brief was even printed in *al-Muḥāmāh* and given wide publicity.[21] When the court found that the law obtaining at the time gave the lawyers no such immunity, the board hastened to correct this deficiency in a new draft of the Advocates Law.[22] In the remaining two incidents the accused, defended by the bar on appeal, were found not guilty.

The close attention given by the bar to these cases served to impress upon judges and lawyers alike that advocates perform a necessary function in the judicial process and that they should not be hindered in its performance.[23] After an altercation in 1946 between the president of the Cairo district court and three defense lawyers over the refusal of the judge to put into the record all that transpired in the sitting, an extraordinary session of the bar was immediately ordered to look into the incident. Even though the judge, accompanied by a counselor at the court of appeal and the chief of the Attorney General's office in Cairo, called at the bar association building to express his regrets, the general assembly of the bar passed strong resolutions in support of a lawyer's sacred right of defense.[24] In 1949, when the immunity of a lawyer from conviction for contempt of court at the scene of the original trial came under attack in a law-revision

[21] *Al-Muḥāmāh,* vol. 10, no. 1.

[22] The provision is now found in Article 52 of Law 96 for the year 1957.

[23] *Minutes,* part I, pp. 68–67, 42.

[24] *Minutes,* part II, pp. 408–407.

committee of the Senate during the authoritarian rule of Ibrāhīm ʻAbd-al-Hādi (December, 1948, to July, 1949), the general assembly of the bar passed a strong resolution in support of immunity and denounced the efforts of the committee to empower the judge, instead of the Attorney General, to commit the lawyer to trial.[25]

The first important incident in the conflict between the bar and the Council of Ministers came in the wake of the suspension of the Egyptian Constitution on July 19, 1928. The constitutional Wafdist government of Musṭafa al-Naḥḥās had been dismissed, and a new ministry had been formed on June 27 by Muḥammad Maḥmūd of the Liberal Constitutionalists, who hastened to suspend the Constitution of 1923, dissolve the parliament, and rule the country with an iron hand. In its enthusiasm to stifle all opposition and damage the reputation of its opponents, the ministry committed to trial before the Disciplinary Council former Premier al-Naḥḥās and two lawyer colleagues on a trumped-up charge of "violating the honor of their profession." When the council declared them innocent of the charge, the ministry expressed its ire by decreeing a change in the Advocates Law of 1912 whereby the disciplining of lawyers was placed in the hands of the chamber of cassation in its capacity as a disciplinary council, instead of the old Disciplinary Council, which included a representative of the bar. The decree further stipulated that disciplinary trials were to be held *in camera.*[26] No sooner was this decree issued than the general assembly of the bar was convened on February 28, 1929, in extraordinary session to protest it. The report of the board to the general assembly denounced the decree as providing the "executive authorities with the opportunity to fight the lawyers among their political opponents through the constant interference with their profession."[27] In its resolution on

[25] *Minutes,* part II, p. 285. See footnote 22 above for the present provision.

[26] See ʻAbd al-Raḥmān Rāfiʻi, *Fi Aʻqāb,* vol. II, Cairo, 1947, pp. 75–76, and Decree 16 for the year 1929.

[27] *Minutes,* part I, p. 74.

this point the general assembly condemned the efforts to exclude the representative of the bar from the disciplinary body, branded the decree unconstitutional in that it was not a result of the normal legislative process, and called for a one-week strike by all lawyers to protest the actions of the government.[28] In the years that followed there were further amendments and counteramendments to the Advocates Law, reflecting the political turbulence of the period, until the law was finally recodified in 1939.[29]

During the ministry of 'Abd al-Fattāḥ Yaḥya (September, 1933, to November, 1934), and following a succession of cabinets which failed to resolve the central issue of a treaty with Britain, the government followed the same system of repression pursued earlier by Ismā'īl Ṣidqi's government (1930 to 1933). The bar association was especially made the object of persecution because some of the government's political opponents had been elected to the board. On December 14, 1933, the government had issued a statement—a copy of which was sent to the president of the bar on the eve of its yearly meeting—that it had been intimated to the government that some lawyers were about to nominate for election to the board some of their colleagues who two days previously had been reprimanded by the chamber of cassation for withdrawing in anger from a court trying their clients for political crimes; that the government urged the general assembly not to elect these lawyers; and that if it did elect them, the government would be obliged forthwith to issue a law voiding their election. The general assembly, completely beside itself for the "unjustifiable interference of the government in its elections," ignored the warning and elected three lawyers who had been disciplined, including the new president, Makram 'Ubayd, a prominent Wafdist. In the face of this challenge, the government pushed through the parliament its threatened law,[30] which made it illegal to elect to the board of the bar a lawyer who had been disciplined and ex-

[28] *Minutes,* part I, pp. 72–71.
[29] Amended again in 1944 and recodified in 1957.
[30] Law 86 for the year 1933, dated December 28, 1933.

tended the ban to include the current board members, a retroactive measure in complete violation of basic constitutional provisions. The general assembly met again on January 26, 1934, and resolved unanimously that there was no need to elect three new members to the board, since a retroactive law was unconstitutional. The government was to have its way, however, and issued a decree on July 5, 1934, suspending those provisions in the Advocates Law which established the National Bar Association and appointing a committee of two judges and the Attorney General to safeguard its assets. The board, nevertheless continued to consider itself the legal representative of the lawyers until the anomaly was settled; on December 20, 1934, the new ministry of Muḥammad Tawfīq Nasīm abolished this decree and called for a new election, which returned Makram 'Ubayd to the presidency—a victory not only for 'Ubayd, but also for the dignity and inviolability of the bar.[31]

There were also occasions on which the lawyers themselves were not sufficiently responsible to maintain the dignity of the bar, a failing which invited the interference of the government. When lawyers could not agree on a board toward the end of 1939, a decree issued by the ministry of 'Ali Māhir (August, 1939 to June, 1940) appointed one representing all political parties in the country.[32] In December, 1942, after the expulsion of Makram 'Ubayd from the Wafdist government (February, 1942 to October 1944) and from the Wafd Party itself, a spirited contest took place at a meeting of the general assembly between 'Ubayd and the nominee of the Wafd Party, Maḥmūd Basyūni, for the presidency. When chairs started flying across the assembly hall the police had to interfere to keep order![33]

[31] For the entire incident see Rāfi'i, pp. 183–188; *Minutes,* part II, pp. 796–794, 789–781, 772–771.

[32] 'Abd al-Raḥmān Rāfi'i, *Mudhakkirāti,* Cairo, 1952, pp. 110–111.

[33] *Minutes,* part II, p. 525. Makram 'Ubayd, who had been the Minister of Finance in the Wafdist government and a close col-

In the aftermath of World War II the question of a new treaty with Britain brought about increased tension in the political life of the country. Lawyers and the bar association were especially active in opposing a treaty which did not realize all national demands. Perhaps it was this activity that caused both the Ismā'īl Ṣidqi and the Maḥmūd Fahmi al-Nuqrāshi governments to attempt, in 1946 and 1947, respectively, to amend the Advocates Law of 1944 in a manner that would better control the vociferous elements of the bar. The second government in particular attempted to dissipate the power of the bar by proposing to create three separate bars in Cairo, Alexandria, and Asyūṭ, to deprive lawyers who were admitted only to the courts of first instance, the young and energetic lawyers, from attending the general assembly, and to limit the membership of the board to those who had been practicing for ten years or more, a measure also directed against the young lawyers.[34] The bar association, however, vehemently resisted the change, and the events of the Palestine war and the Army revolt of 1952 kept the whole question in abeyance until 1957, when only mild modifications were introduced into the Advocates Law.[35]

SHARĪ'AH COURTS AND BAR ASSOCIATION

The developments that embraced the mixed and the national courts in the late 1900s naturally prepared the way for the reorganization of the courts dealing primarily with personal

---

laborator of its Premier, Muṣṭafa al-Naḥḥās, aroused the ire of the latter when in May, 1942, he opposed the exceptional promotion of certain Wafdist civil servants on the ground that such action would be demoralizing to the entire cadre. The animosity between the two men was further aggravated when 'Ubayd refused to accord preferential treatment to some in-laws of Naḥḥās in the granting of export licenses. Upon 'Ubayd's refusal to resign, Naḥḥās reconstituted his cabinet without him. In July 'Ubayd was expelled from the Wafd Party.

[34] *Minutes,* part II, pp. 393–388, 365–361.

[35] Law 96 for the year 1957.

status among Muslims, the *sharīʿah* courts. These courts, it will be remembered, had been the ordinary courts of the country, with a jurisdiction which theoretically embraced every type of case, both civil and criminal. In 1882, in his memorandum on the reorganization of the national courts,[36] Ḥusayn Fakhri Pasha had called for limiting the jurisdiction of the *sharīʿah* courts to questions of personal status and even for depriving them of dealing with cases of murder, which until that time were tried concurrently in the *sharīʿah* courts (for blood money) and the provincial councils.[37] Serious reorganization was not undertaken until May 27, 1897, when a decree was issued setting up three levels of courts and defining the jurisdiction of each in questions of personal status only. From then on the jurisdiction of these courts no longer depended upon the *sharīʿah,* but upon statute. The state even took some steps to infuse new life into the *sharīʿah* courts. Up to that time they had been composed solely of *ulema* who had diplomas from al-Azhar University or equivalent certificates. Realizing that such traditional training was not adequate for an efficient court system, the authorities looked for ways and means of improving that training. The report of the Judicial Adviser for the year 1905 explained these efforts:[38]

> We have lately had under consideration a project for the establishment of a Training College for Cadis [Qāḍis] on the lines of that which has been established by the Austrian government at Sarajevo [Bosnia] and had proved a decided success. . . . The school would educate men for judicial and other posts in the Mehkemehs [*sharīʿah* courts]. The candidates would be chosen from among the students of al-Azhar and they would receive instruction in such practical matters as the drawing up of *procés verbaux* and judgements; the organization and procedure of the Mehkemehs, the regulations in force, administrative law, etc.

[36] Discussed in Chapter 2.

[37] *Al-Kitāb al-Dhahabi lil-Maḥākim al-Ahliyyah,* vol. I, Cairo, 1937, p. 113.

[38] *Report of the Judicial Adviser for the Year* 1905, p. 46.

> A committee under the late Grand Mufti [Muḥammad 'Abduh] . . . was appointed to draw up the regulations and curriculum of such a school. The committee completed its labors last June. . . . The course of education was to be of a liberal character, not confined to purely religious studies.

The school came into being in 1907, following the appointment of Sa'd Zaghlūl as Minister of Education. His enthusiasm for the school dissipated the opposition of the Khedive and those conservative elements who had felt that this measure would detract from the traditional standing of al-Azhar.[39] The report of the Judicial Adviser for the year 1916 praised the educational methods followed at the school and its wholesome influence upon reformist tendencies at al-Azhar, of which it was regarded as forming a part.[40]

The *qāḍi* school provided not only judges and clerks for the *sharī'ah* courts, but also advocates to plead before them. Article 76 of the decree which established the courts limited representation in actions before them to *muḥāmūn,* those *wukalā'* who were at the time also practicing before the other courts. When the affairs of advocates pleading before the national courts were set in order in 1912, however, it was not long before some voices were heard clamoring for similar measures with regard to advocates pleading before the *sharī'ah* courts. The result was Law 15 for the year 1916, which set out in detail the rights and duties of those advocates. According to this law, the *sharī'ah* advocates were to be placed on a footing similar to that of the national advocates in matters of admission

[39] 'Abbās Maḥmūd al-'Aqqād, *Sa'd Zaghlūl,* Cairo, 1936, pp. 120–121.

[40] *Report of the Judicial Adviser for the Year* 1916, pp. 30–31. The school was first under the jurisdiction of the Ministry of Education, then the High Azhar Council, then the Ministry of Justice, and finally again the Ministry of Education. It was abolished in 1923, reactivated in 1927, and finally dissolved in 1929. Interview with Shaykh M. Abu Zahrah.

to the bar, *stage*, discipline, and, last but not least, the formation of a bar association on lines akin to those of the National Bar Association. In the matter of admission to the Sharī'ah Bar Association not only were graduates of the Cairo Law School eligible, but also those persons holding the diploma of *'ālimiyyah* from any of the schools of al-Azhar, in addition to those who were eligible because of previous service as judges in the *sharī'ah* courts.[41]

The Sharī'ah Bar was never able to gain the same prestige as the National Bar. In the first place, its members for the most part did not have as high a level of education. In the second place, the practice of the *sharī'ah* advocates was limited to matters of personal status, a field of law which was not, except for *waqf* cases, as lucrative or as commanding of respect as other fields of law. The really decisive factor in this lack of prestige was the fact that the *sharī'ah* advocates were the defenders of a religious order that was constantly giving way to secular ideas and progressive legislation. The defensive position of the *sharī'ah* advocates can be gleaned from the stand they took against many measures that were considered by secular elements as proper and progressive. A perusal of the minutes of the bar meetings reveals those advocates as thoroughly conservative, especially when conservatism preserved their own financial interests.[42]

In controversies that pertained to religious or quasi-religious matters *sharī'ah* advocates tended to rigidity and reaction. In 1936, when the Egyptian Council of Ministers approved a proposal advanced by the rector of al-Azhar to have the council of al-Azhar undertake, with the assistance of the Ministry of Education, the "translation of the meanings of the glorious Koran in an official translation" to other languages, the Sharī'ah Bar

[41] Article 2 of Law 15 for the year 1916.

[42] The minutes of the Sharī'ah Bar meetings for the years 1916 to 1928 have, unfortunately, been lost. The minutes for the years 1928 to 1954 were placed for safekeeping at the Ministry of Finance in Cairo following the abolishment of that bar.

protested violently against such a translation and dubbed it as "violating religion and enticing people away from memorizing the Book of Almighty God in the language in which it was revealed."[43] Two years later the Sharīʿah bar demanded that the authorities "propagate Muslim religious education throughout the government schools inasmuch as the religion of the state is Islam."[44]

Appeals to religion were sometimes also utilized in fighting the inroads into the jurisdiction of the *sharīʿah* courts, and hence the livelihood of its advocates. In this situation religious appeals were more relevant, since much of the jurisdiction of *sharīʿah* courts, especially matters of personal status, was bound up with religion. In 1937, for instance, the Sharīʿah Bar did battle on three measures which threatened the legal practice of its members. One was Article 293 of the Penal Code, which granted the national and mixed courts the right to deal with cases of imprisonment for nonpayment of alimony and maintenance, a personal-status matter; the other was the transfer of the function of the *ḥisbiyyah* councils, the courts of wards,[45] to the national courts rather than the *Sharīʿah* courts; and the third was a proposal to do away with family *waqfs* (religious endowments primarily for the constitutor's family). During a debate on the subject a prominent *sharīʿah* advocate was quoted as saying: "Sharīʿah Courts are the most important manifestation of the Muslim state; Sharīʿah advocates, in their capacity as men of religion, look at these questions not from a financial, but from a religious point of view."[46]

The army revolt of July 23, 1952, with its distinctly reformist tendencies and secular approach, caused both direct and

[43] S. Mahmassani, *Falsafat al-Tashrīʿ fī al-Islām* (tr. by F. J. Ziadeh as *The Philosophy of Jurisprudence in Islam*), Leiden, 1961, pp. 68–69; Sharīʿah Bar minutes for June 12, 1936.

[44] *Minutes of the Sharīʿah Bar Association,* May 13, 1938.

[45] For the composition and jurisdiction of these courts see J. Y. Brinton, *The Mixed Courts of Egypt, New Haven, Conn.,* 1930, pp. 283–284.

[46] *Minutes of the Sharīʿah Bar Association,* August 20, 1937.

indirect pressure on the *sharīʿah* courts and, by extension, the Sharīʿah Bar. No sooner was the Revolutionary Command Council in power than a law was issued abolishing family *waqfs,* which accounted for the major part of litigation before the *sharīʿah* courts.[47] The *sharīʿah* advocates saw the handwriting on the wall and marshaled forces to safeguard their livelihoods. In a memorandum to the authorities setting forth their demands, which were later reemphasized in the form of resolutions passed at a meeting of the bar, they called for an enlarged jurisdiction for the *sharīʿah* courts over all *waqf* and personal-status matters and insisted that the jurisdiction of those courts over charitable *waqfs* (religious endowments for charitable purposes) not be curtailed, a reflection of their fear that such a step was being contemplated.[48]

A far more serious matter was soon to face the *sharīʿah* advocates. A subcommittee of the Constitutional Committee, which was formulating principles for a new constitution, approved the principle of unifying the judiciary by merging the *sharīʿah* courts with the national courts. The *sharīʿah* advocates, fearing a complete loss of their practice because of their ineligibility to plead before the national courts, were up in arms against such a principle and pleaded with the President of the Republic, the ministers, and the rector of al-Azhar to use their authority and influence to block such a proposal. One advocate even suggested the completely anachronistic proposal of accepting the principle of unifying the judiciary on condition that Islamic law be the only law applicable in the country.[49]

In the period of uncertainty which followed *sharīʿah* advocates came forward with a variety of haphazard proposals to save their practice. One was to deny admission to their bar to new candidates for a period of two years; another was to deny the national advocates the right to plead before the *sharīʿah* courts, a right even non-Muslim national advocates had availed them-

[47] Law 180 for the year 1952.
[48] *Minutes of the Sharīʿah Bar Association,* April 23, 1953.
[49] *Minutes of the Sharīʿah Bar Association,* January 15, 1954.

selves of; a third was to permit the *sharīʿah* advocates to plead before the national courts in matters pertaining to personal status.[50] Finally, the matter was put at rest when Law 462 for the year 1955 abolished the *sharīʿah* courts and other confessional courts entirely and assigned their work as of January 1, 1956, to the national courts, and when Law 625 for the year 1955 granted *sharīʿah* advocates the right to plead in all matters before the national courts. The only remaining difference between the national and the *sharīʿah* advocates was that *sharīʿah* advocates were to be allowed to plead before the Court of Cassation only in matters which formerly had been within the exclusive jurisdiction of the *sharīʿah* courts.[51] The generous treatment accorded the *sharīʿah* advocates was ascribed by them to President Nasser personally, and seems to have been based on political rather than legal considerations.[52]

[50] *Minutes of the Sharīʿah Bar Association,* April 9, October 15, 1954.

[51] Article 3 of Law 625 for the year 1955.

[52] In an interview in April, 1958, Shaykh ʿAbd al Razzāq al-Qāḍi, the first and last president of the Sharīʿah Bar, said: "President Nasser gave us the right to plead before the National Courts. When we went to Aḥmad Ḥusni, the Minister of Justice, to thank him for granting us that right, he refused to accept our thanks and said that he had not agreed to the measure in the first place." Apparently, by this measure President Nasser wanted to win over the support of conservative elements represented by the Sharīʿah advocates.

CHAPTER FOUR

lawyers and nationalist action

The complete failure of the ʿArābi revolt and the disintegration of its leadership, the British occupation of Egypt and the loss of its autonomy, and the submissiveness and resignation of the former leaders resulted in a general attitude of despondency. The military leadership had been discredited, and the army was reorganized under British command. The Azharite elements that had supported the revolt were now either "cooperative" with the British authorities or completely ineffectual; moreover, al-Azhar could no longer attract the scions of distinguished families to its ranks because of the competition of secular schools run along modern lines.[1] The time was ripe, therefore, for the emer-

[1] For instance, the three distinguished lawyers and national leaders ʿAbd al-ʿAzīz Fahmi, Aḥmad Luṭfi al-Sayyid, and ʿAbd al-

gence of a completely different kind of leadership, a leadership that depended primarily on political action along secular lines and could, in view of the internationalization of the Egyptian question following the British occupation, establish extensive contacts in Europe in anticipation of explaining the Egyptian problem to world public opinion. Such a leadership was supplied by rising generations of young lawyers who had studied either in French universities or in the Egyptian Law School. The pioneer in this leadership was Muṣṭafa Kāmil (1874–1908), the father of modern Egyptian nationalism.[2]

Kāmil's interest in nationalism—which at that time meant working for the freedom and independence of Egypt—seems to have started rather early. While he was still in high school he organized a thriving literary society that evidenced nationalist sentiments. Upon finishing high school he wrote to a brother of his intention to join the Egyptian Law School because it was "the school for writing, oratory, and the ascertainment of the rights of individuals and nations." After one year there he concurrently joined the French Law School, then conducting classes in Cairo to prepare students for examinations held in France, to strengthen his French language for the purpose of defending the Egyptian cause in European circles. At the same time he wrote several articles for the local papers dealing with nationalist subjects and often delivered speeches to his fellow students on freedom and national independence. He even established a

Raḥmān al-Rāfi'i were slated to study at al-Azhar but instead chose secular schools. See the memoirs of Fahmi and al-Sayyid in *al-Muṣawwar,* June 10, 1949, and September 1, 1950, respectively, and the memoirs of al-Rāfi'i in 'Abd al-Raḥmān al-Rāfi'i, *Mudhakkirāti,* Cairo, 1952, p. 9.

This chapter presents only the role of lawyers in nationalist action. For a thorough treatment of Egyptian political developments during the first half of this century see John Marlowe, *Anglo-Egyptian Relations,* 1800–1953, London, 1954, or Jacob M. Landau, *Parliaments and Parties in Egypt,* Tel-Aviv, 1953.

[2] For a complete biography, including Kāmil's political activities, see 'Abd al-Raḥmān al-Rāfi'i, *Muṣṭafa Kāmil,* Cairo, 1950.

monthly school magazine called *al-Madrasah* (*The School*) to further that aim and assumed both its management and editorship. His trips to France in 1893 and 1894 for his examinations put him in touch with French journalists and publicists, who doubtless must have influenced his ideas on patriotism and love of one's country. No sooner had he obtained his law degree from Toulouse University than he wrote his brother of his intention to become an advocate "to defend the rights of individuals, and if I were given a chance . . . to defend the rights of the entire nation, because Egypt, the paradise of the world, does not deserve to have its honor trodden upon."[3]

When Kāmil returned to Egypt in December, 1894, he had his name inscribed on the roll of advocates, but he never practiced law. Instead, he devoted his entire energy to the study and defense of the Egyptian cause in the press and in interviews and contacts with important foreign personages. He traveled several times to Paris and other European capitals in attempts to convince European public opinion through speeches and articles of Egypt's right for independence and of the harm he felt the British occupation was causing both to Egypt and to European interests in general.[4]

In January 1900 Kāmil began publishing *al-Liwā'* (the *Standard*), a daily newspaper which gradually attracted the nationalist elements and became a school for patriotism, teaching Egyptians their rights and duties and indoctrinating them with the ideas of liberty and self-rule. By 1905 the widespread feeling of resignation and submission in Egypt had started to give way to a new awakening to nationalist ends. The first concrete evidence of this was the establishment that year of the Higher Schools Club, with membership drawn from the students and graduates of the schools of medicine, law, engineering, and education and languages. This club, in addition to sponsoring many social and sporting activities, was instrumental in fostering

[3] Al-Rāfi'i, *Kāmil*, pp. 25, 34, 41.
[4] Al-Rāfi'i, *Kāmil*, pp. 43–44.

the nationalist principles enunciated by Kāmil.[5] Another evidence was the strike the students of the Egyptian Law School carried out in February 1906 against the Ministry of Education, which, upon the advice of its British Secretary-General, had announced new regulations placing its students in many respects on the same footing as high school students. This strike was the first of its kind, for it involved an entire school of higher education and was understood to be directed against a policy inspired by the authorities of occupation. According to E. Lambert, the French jurist who headed the Egyptian Law School later in the same year, the ministry's action transformed the school into a stronghold for Egyptian nationalism, so much so that of the 400 students there were no more than ten who did not avow the principles of Muṣṭafa Kāmil.[6]

In this initial period of awakening nationalism, on June 13, 1906, an event took place which rocked the entire country and set it astir with resentment and indignation against the occupying power. This was the Denshiway incident, in which one British army officer was killed and three others were wounded in a fight with Egyptian peasants following a shooting accident in which an Egyptian woman was wounded by one of the soldiers. In the trial that followed four peasants were sentenced to death and many others received sentences of varying severity. The fact that a special court, with no appeal from its sentences, had tried the defendants, that the trial was conducted with the utmost speed, that the sentences were harsh, and that the trial was conducted in an atmosphere of intimidation served to convince the Egyptians that the occupation authorities were out to teach them a lesson.[7]

Kāmil, who was in Europe at the time, made the most of this incident in Paris and London, appealing to the conscience of humanity to censure the British occupation of Egypt. On

[5] Al-Rāfi'i, *Kāmil,* pp. 143ff, 188–191.

[6] Al-Rāfi'i, *Kāmil,* p. 193.

[7] For this incident see al-Rāfi'i, *Kāmil,* pp. 197ff; Marlowe, pp. 168–170.

his return to Cairo he found that the rank and file of articulate Egyptians were in support of his nationalist movement. This support had some important results. One was the attention paid to the Egyptian problem by the world press. Another was a change in the British policy in Egypt, whereby the policy of repression was replaced by one of compromise, with important ministerial posts filled by prominent Egyptians with grass-roots popularity. The appointment on October 26, 1906, of Sa'd Zaghlūl as Minister of Education and the resignation in April, 1907, of Baring, then Lord Cromer, the British High Commissioner, were indications of that policy. A third result, indirect but nonetheless real, was the feeling that some constructive step should be taken to raise the intellectual standard of Egypt and prepare it for independence. This feeling was given form when a group headed by Sa'd Zaghlūl and Qāsim Amīn, both at the time judges in the Court of Appeal, organized on October 12, 1906, a committee for the establishment of the Egyptian University.[8] The Egyptian nationalist movement was now well on its way, and in December, 1907, the Nationalist Party was formed under the leadership of Muṣṭafa Kāmil. As fate would have it, he died two months later, leaving a close friend and confidant, Muḥammad Farīd, in command of the party.

Farīd, like Kamīl, had been trained as a lawyer. After graduation from the Egyptian Law School in 1887 he worked for the law department of the khedivial estates and then was transferred to the Attorney General's office, where he later became a deputy attorney general at the Court of Appeal. While in that office he openly expressed his nationalist sentiments, especially in support of an editor of a nationalist newspaper who was being tried for violating state secrets in publishing telegrams from Lord Kitchener, the Commander-in-Chief of the Egyptian Army in the Sudan, to the War Ministry in Cairo about the prosecution of the war against the Dervishes and the incidence of cholera among his troops. When the editor was exon-

[8] Al-Rāfi'i, *Kāmil*, pp. 232–238.

erated, Farīd was transferred to a remote post in Upper Egypt. Officialdom in Cairo interpreted this transfer as an expression of disfavor by the occupation authorities. Farīd considered it a move affecting the independence of the judicial process and offered his resignation, which was immediately accepted. He then joined the ranks of the advocates—to the chagrin of his aristocratic father, who considered the calling of advocate far below the proper standing of his son[9]—and practiced law for seven years. In 1904 he left this profession to devote his energies to the nationalist movement, which was being led by his friend Muṣṭafa Kāmil. Upon assumption of the leadership of the Nationalist Party after Kāmil's death, Farīd insisted on implementation of the party's slogan, complete evacuation of the British from Egypt and the establishment of constitutional government.[10] To this end he continued Kāmil's activities both in Egypt and abroad, and called a conference in Brussels in September, 1910, to support Egypt's right for independence. His constant harassment by the authorities, however, forced him to leave Egypt in 1912 and remain in exile until his death in 1919.[11]

Late in 1908 some hopes were entertained that constitutional government and parliamentary rule might be favorably viewed by the incoming government. The outgoing ministry of Muṣṭafa Fahmi Pasha, which had been in power for thirteen years and was completely subservient to the British authorities, had opposed such measures. When the new ministry, headed by Buṭrus Pasha Ghāli, assumed power, Farīd, noting that four of its members, including Sa'd Zaghlūl, were lawyers, welcomed it in an article in *al-Liwā'*: "Four of the ministers hold high diplomas in the legal sciences. . . . In its totality the present ministry is the best that can be hoped for in Egypt. . . . Its members are constitutionalists who have not been accustomed to the old regime when a single individual assumed absolute

[9] See the discussion in Chapter Two.

[10] See 'Abd al-Raḥmān al-Rāfi'i, *Muḥammad Farīd,* Cairo, 1950, pp. 18–42.

[11] Al-Rāfi'i, *Farīd,* pp. 191, 274, 370.

power."[12] Those hopes were dashed, however, when it became apparent that in these matters Ghāli's new ministry was no improvement over its predecessor.

The question of constitutional government, which was a constant issue, was raised in an unusual manner in March, 1910. At that time United States President Theodore Roosevelt, who was traveling through Africa, gave a lecture at the Egyptian University in which he implicitly deprecated the efforts of the Egyptians to obtain a constitution, saying that to be eligible for self-government a nation needed generations of training, and not merely a written constitution. His remarks stirred up a hornet's nest. The Nationalist Party immediately protested and held a demonstration in support of the constitution and independence. 'Abd al-Raḥmān al-Rāfi'i and two other advocates, who were then practicing in Zaqāzīq, sent Mr. Roosevelt a courteous, but strong, letter arguing that Egypt was ready for self-government and that the nationalist stand was basically the same as that of the United States in having rebelled against the British in 1776.[13]

The position of the legal profession was marred, however, when a group of lawyers, in their enthusiasm for proper legal defense, raised a political assassin to the rank of national hero, thereby indirectly encouraging other would-be assassins who later plagued Egyptian politics. On February 20, 1910, Ibrāhīm N. Wirdāni, a pharmacist, shot and killed Prime Minister Buṭrus Pasha Ghāli. The assassin readily admitted the crime, but said that he had been impelled to commit it because of Ghāli's so-called treacherous acts in signing the Sudan Convention of 1889,[14] in heading the Denshiway trials, in restricting the liberty of the press, and in striving to prolong the Suez Canal concession. Advocate Ibrāhīm al-Hilbāwi, who outdid himself in his defense (perhaps to atone for having conducted the prosecution

[12] Quoted in al-Rāfi'i, *Farīd,* pp. 80–81.

[13] For the entire incident see al-Rāfi'i, *Farīd,* pp. 160–163.

[14] For this convention, which set up the Anglo-Egyptian condominium over the Sudan, see Marlowe, pp. 159, 409–411.

in the Denshiway trials), emphasized the national sentiments of the defendant and couched his defense in ringing literary terms. In a volatile political milieu this defense had unfortunate repercussions.[15]

Up to and during World War I the participation of lawyers in the nationalist movement had, on the whole, been an individual affair. It was after the war that advocates as a group started to make themselves felt as the leading force in the general call for independence and constitutional government. Sa'd Zaghlūl, who had resigned his ministerial post after a fight with Lord Kitchener, the British High Commissioner, started to regain the popularity he had lost as a minister, especially after he was elected deputy to the newly created but short-lived Legislative Council early in 1914 and assumed the role of leader of the opposition in it. It followed that he was the most prominent member of the *wafd,* or delegation, formed on November 13, 1918, to plead the cause of independence for Egypt, especially at the Paris Peace Conference and at the Foreign Office in London.[16] It was also natural that this *wafd,* which after many hardships was finally allowed to travel to Paris in April, 1919, included six lawyers[17] among its sixteen members, a recognition of their ability and of the prominent role they had played in the rebellion the preceding month.

The rebellion had been triggered when, on March 8, 1919, the British authorities exiled four leaders of the *wafd* to Malta for political agitation, which was considered embarrassing to the government. The initial demonstrations had ended in bloody clashes with the British police and troops. Students went on strike, as they had often done when their feelings were aroused,

[15] For the details of the trial see Maḥmūd 'Āṣim, *al-Murāfa'āt fi Ashhar al-Qaḍāyā,* Cairo, 1933–1935, pp. 81–226; for al-Hilbāwi's defense see 'Abd al-Ḥalīm al-Jundi, *al-Hilbāwi,* Cairo, n.d., pp. 46–50.

[16] 'Abbās Maḥmūd al-'Aqqād, *Sa'd Zaghlūl,* Cairo, 1936, pp. 158–196.

[17] Sa'd Zaghlūl, 'Abd al-'Azīz Fahmi, Aḥmad Luṭfi al-Sayyid, Muḥammad 'Ali 'Allūbah, Muṣṭafa al-Naḥḥās, and Maḥmūd Abu-al-Naṣr.

but when the advocates went on strike it was a clarion call for all professional and trade groups to follow suit because of the prestige advocates had acquired as defenders of national rights.[18] This strike brought the judicial process almost to a standstill, and the Deputy Judicial Adviser threatened the advocates with strong measures if they did not return to work. In answer the board of the bar association insisted that "the Bar, which is cognizant of its standing, cannot desist from showing its distaste for the events which [are] taking place." To the charge that the interests of the litigants were being sacrificed in the strike, the board retorted that "the interests of litigants, which you are so concerned about, also concern us; and it is these interests themselves which motivated us to protest in this way."[19]

The rebellion moved the British government to release the exiled leaders and to allow the *wafd* to proceed to Paris. Later in the year the British appointed a commission headed by Lord Milner to investigate the causes of the rebellion and to effect a compromise between Egyptian aspirations and British interests. However, the Egyptians, perhaps impressed by the fact that Lord Milner was the Colonial Secretary, viewed the commission as an instrument for establishing the protectorate on a permanent basis, or even for turning Egypt into a colony.[20] This apprehension was evident in a resolution adopted by the general assembly of the bar on December 12, 1919. The resolution, after protesting the fact that several lawyers had been sentenced for their political activities and others were being held for trial, asserted that the legal profession was a force to be respected and that it was because of the measures taken against the advocates and "for the grave circumstances obtaining at the time, especially the impending arrival of the Lord Milner Commission, which is a new manifestation of aggression against the independence of

[18] 'Abd al-Raḥmān al-Rāfi'i, *Thawrat Sanat* 1919, Cairo, 1946, pp. 132–134.

[19] *Minutes of the General Assembly of the National Bar Association,* part I, p. 222.

[20] See al-'Aqqād, p. 288.

Egypt and which has the aim of confirming the British protectorate," that the general assembly called for a strike by all lawyers. The strike was to last for one week.[21]

The sojourn of the Milner Commission in Egypt, its return to London, its negotiations with the *wafd* there, and the inconclusive character of the negotiations are not relevant here. But when in 1921 the time came for the British government to invite the Sultan of Egypt to send an official delegation to negotiate a political settlement between Britain and Egypt, the board of the bar sided with the nationalist elements which supported Zaghlūl and maintained that it would be inopportune for Egypt to enter into negotiations with the British without first agreeing on the bases and conditions of such negotiations. Although some thirty-four lawyers, presumably representing the government point of view, which favored the initiation of negotiations, demanded that the general assembly convene to vote on the decision of the board, the board stuck to its position.[22] This is surprising, in view of the large moderate elements among the lawyers, and can be explained only by the forceful personality of Zaghlūl, who demanded that he personally preside over the delegation and that certain primary bases for negotiations be set.

Following the failure of the negotiations which Premier 'Adli Yegen Pasha conducted with the British government in London in 1920, and the subsequent closing of ranks among the various Egyptian groups, the British authorities inaugurated a policy of repression. Zaghlūl and five associates, including lawyers Muṣṭafa al-Naḥḥās and Makram 'Ubayd, were exiled in December, 1921, to the Seychelles. Then, in January, 1922, Murqus Ḥanna, the president of the bar, and some of his colleagues, who had taken the place of the exiled leaders in the Wafd Party, were arrested, released, and rearrested because of their political activities. In the military-court trial that followed they were first condemned to death, but the sentence was commuted to seven years' imprisonment and a heavy fine. As was expected, the arrest

[21] *Minutes*, part I, p. 217.
[22] *Minutes*, part I, p. 200.

and trial aroused the board of the bar, which protested to King Fuad against "the interference of a foreign authority in a country which is said to be completely independent."[23] The board asserted in a legalistic fashion that the country had courts and laws, and that if someone were charged with violating those laws, then its courts had exclusive jurisdiction over the matter. In December the board sent a delegation to the King in Alexandria to complain again about the actions of the British military authorities. This delegation presented a petition requesting that he interfere "to save the country, to restore to those exiled or arrested their liberty, and to put an end to martial law, so that . . . the rule of law be established.[24]

Meanwhile, the moderate ʻAbd al-Khāliq Tharwat Pasha, who as chief prosecutor had opposed al-Hilbāwi's radical defense in the Wirdāni trial and had been largely responsible for convincing the British authorities to grant Egypt its independence while reserving four contested issues for future negotiation,[25] formed a government to succeed that of ʻAdli Pasha on March 1, 1922. Tharwat was an able and diplomatic politician,[26] but he did not find much favor with the bar, which at that time was in complete support of Zaghlūl and the Wafdists. In the first place, the board of the bar declared in a resolution passed on February 8, 1922, that the conditions set by Tharwat for the formation of a government did not justify that action in the circumstances obtaining at the time. In the second place, it deprecated his efforts to form a committee to draw up a constitution for the country. Not only did the president of the bar refuse to join the committee when he was invited to do so, but the board adopted a resolution on April 5, 1922, in support of his refusal, declaring

[23] The reference here is to the "independence" granted the country in a British declaration dated February 28, 1922. The title of the ruler of the country was changed from "Sultan" to "King."

[24] *Minutes,* part I, pp. 187, 186.

[25] See Marlowe, p. 248.

[26] See, for instance, Muḥammad Ḥusayn Haykal, *Tarājim Miṣriyyah wa-Gharbiyyah,* Cairo, n.d., pp. 204–208.

that any lawyer or past president of the bar who might join the committee would be doing so only in a personal capacity, and not as a representative of the advocates in general. The justification for this stand was that "the writing of a constitution is a right belonging to the nation, because it is the appropriate entity to define its authority and the responsibility of the government to it. . . . The nation should be represented in this question by a national assembly chosen in a free election not affected by martial law or the influence of the administrative authorities."[27] Nevertheless, a committee of thirty completed the task of writing the Constitution and presented its draft to Tharwat on October 18, 1922. However, a wave of political crime and violence forced him to resign on November 30 in the hope that the constitutional measures would be eventually completed.[28]

When the Constitution of Egypt was finally promulgated on April 19, 1923, the country prepared for elections. Zaghlūl was released from exile, and the Wafd Party won an overwhelming majority of the seats in the House of Representatives in one of the fairest elections in Egypt. It was evident then that Zaghlūl would head the first constitutional government, which included three other prominent lawyers who received the congratulations of the bar in a special resolution passed by its general assembly.[29]

The assassination by extremist elements in Cairo of Sir Lee Stack, the Sirdar of the Egyptian Army and Governor General of the Sudan, caused the resignation of the government on November 23, 1924. A British ultimatum addressed to that government contained provisions intended not only to redress the wrong caused by the assassination, but also to achieve certain political aims entirely unrelated to the incident, a situation which the

[27] *Minutes*, part I, p. 185.

[28] Haykal, *Tarājim*, p. 210. Tharwat was the object of two assassination plots. In one of them, according to an interview with the historian ʻAbd al-Raḥmān al-Rafiʻi, the two victims, both prominent members of the Liberal Constitutional Party, were killed by mistake.

[29] *Minutes*, part I, p. 162. The three lawyers were Murqus Ḥanna, Muṣṭafa al-Naḥḥās, and M. Najīb al-Gharābli.

Zaghlūl government found intolerable. Following its resignation and the acceptance by Aḥmad Zīwar's incoming government of all the conditions set by the British, the country was seething with indignation. The general assembly of the bar, in its meeting of December 12, 1924, echoed this feeling in expressing its profound regret for the death of Sir Lee but at the same time protesting the British ultimatum and asserting that compliance with its conditions did not bind the nation. It is interesting to note that on this occasion the general assembly was reluctant to interfere in the political situation owing to "the existence in the country of a representative body," but simply wanted to declare its stand, "which would have its effect on that body."[30] It also seriously limited the right of the board to express political views by insisting that it first approve such views, a measure which the board complained against in its report for the year 1925, especially in view of the need for protest against the violation of the Constitution by the Zīwar government, which twice dissolved the legislature and carried on without it. Perhaps it was this limitation which moved over 300 advocates to complain as a group to King Fuad against the suspension of parliamentary government. In any case, the board itself presented an exhaustive legal report on the subject to the general assembly of the bar, which approved it.[31]

At this time the prominence of lawyers in the nationalist movement was even further enhanced by a series of cases known as the "political-assassination cases." Following the assassination of Sir Lee Stack, the Zīwar government endeavored in investigating crime to discover connections between this and other previous crimes whose victims had also been British. Several prominent Wafdists, including Aḥmad Māhir and Maḥmūd

[30] *Minutes,* part I, p. 157. The same sentiment was echoed in the report of the board a year later: "The convening of Parliament, a body which truly represents the Egyptian people, removed from the shoulders of private organizations, like professional associations, the burden of participating directly in political affairs." *Minutes,* part I, p. 154.

[31] *Minutes,* part I, p. 146; the full report is on pp. 143–138.

Fahmi al-Nuqrāshi, were charged with engineering such crimes and were brought to trial. A battery of the most distinguished lawyers in Egypt came forward to defend them. Only one defendant was found guilty and condemned to death; the others, with Wafd connections, were declared innocent of the charges.[32] The publicity attending the trial, especially after a British judge (Judge Kershaw) presiding over it resigned because of his disagreement with the verdict of his colleagues, imparted further importance to the legal profession as the defender of national causes. The general assembly of the bar, in its meeting of December 17, 1926, even condemned Judge Kershaw for resigning and "violating the tenets of his profession."[33]

Meanwhile, the Zīwar government, under pressure by a coalition of all political parties, had been forced to hold general elections. Although the Wafdists won a majority of the seats, in June, 1926, 'Adli Pasha, a Liberal Constitutionalist, formed a coalition government of Wafdists and men of his own party, including three prominent lawyers. Zaghlūl was elected to the presidency of the Chamber of Deputies, an office he held until his death in 1927. Normal constitutional life had been restored.[34]

On June 25, 1928, the machinations of the Palace and the British, for entirely different purposes, brought about the dismissal from office of another coalition government, this time headed by the Wafdist Muṣṭafa al-Naḥḥās, and the suspension of the Constitution at the hands of a Liberal Constitutional government headed by Muḥammad Maḥmūd. The country's general indignation over the suspension of the Constitution and the dissolution of the parliament for a period of three years was echoed by the general assembly of the bar in its meeting of December 12, 1928, when in a unanimous resolution it decried the "*coup d'état* engineered by the government in suspending the

[32] *Minutes,* part I, p. 130.

[33] For a short account of the trial see 'Abd al-Raḥmān al-Rāfi'i, *Fi A'qāb al-Thawrah al-Miṣriyyah,* Cairo, 1947–1951, vol. I, pp. 259–260.

[34] Al-Rāfi'i, *Fi A'qāb,* p. 263.

Constitution, dismissing Parliament, and stifling the liberties guaranteed by the Constitution."[35]

Although the Constitution was restored in October, 1929, by the government of 'Adli Pasha, who had separated himself from the Liberal Constitutionalists, it was again abolished in October, 1930, by the government of Ismā'īl Ṣidqi Pasha, who substituted a new constitution that negated many of the previously won democratic rights. This constitution was abolished at the end of 1935, thus clearing the way for the restoration of the original Constitution, the resumption of parliamentary life, and the conduct of negotiations with the British toward the conclusion of a treaty defining the relations between the two countries and granting Egypt complete independence. All Egyptian parties except the Nationalist Party participated in these negotiations, and the treaty was concluded on August 26, 1936.[36] The bar, which had struggled hard for the restoration of the Constitution and for complete independence, expressed its jubilance in the report of the board, presented to the general assemby on December 25, 1936.[37]

[35] *Minutes*, part I, p. 94. The lawyers' defense of the constitution against authoritarian attacks is discussed in Chapter 5.

[36] For all these developments see al-Rāfi'i, *Fi A'qāb*, vols. II, III; Marlowe, pp. 281–309.

[37] *Minutes*, part II, p. 752.

CHAPTER FIVE

lawyers as a liberal force

The nationalism of Egyptian lawyers, individually and as a group, was matched, on the whole, by liberalism in many phases of national life. In drawing up the Constitution, defending it against inroads by unscrupulous governments, fighting emergency regulations or martial law, upholding personal freedom (especially for women) and propagating democratic ideas, and in their progressive attitudes toward a myriad national problems, Egyptian lawyers showed an unmistakable liberal bent perhaps attributable to, or at least enhanced by, legal training. Training in law in the early 1900s constituted the primary "liberal education" available to Egyptian students. Little wonder, then, that there was an emphasis on individual rights in many of the situations where a legal stand had to be taken.

The committee appointed to draw up the Constitution of 1923, followed the Belgian constitution[1] but added a whole section dealing with fundamental rights. Egyptians were to be equal before the law, and their personal freedom was to be guaranteed. No person was to be punished or subjected to forced residence except in accordance with the law. Homes, property, and personal correspondence were to be inviolable. Freedom of religion, of opinion, of the press, of speech and of education were to be guaranteed. Finally, Egyptians were to have the right of assembly, of association, and of petition. Some of these freedoms and rights were, of course, subject to legal restrictions.[2] Needless to say, some of the new, liberal provisions conflicted not only with the former autocratic traditions of rule in Egypt, but with the *sharīʿah* itself, which distinguished between Muslims and non-Muslims in many legal institutions.[3]

In the matter of public powers, too, the role of the people and their representatives was emphasized. The nation was declared to be the source of all powers, and the legislative power was to be assumed by the King jointly with the Senate and House of Representatives. No law was to be issued unless it was passed by the legislature and approved by the King.[4] A two-thirds majority of each chamber was enough to override the veto power of the King if a vote were taken again during the same legislative session; a simple majority was sufficient if the vote were taken during the following session.[5] Decrees having the force of law could be issued by the King during a period of emergency when the legislature was not in session, but the leg-

[1] See A. Osman, *Le mouvement constitutionnel en Égypte,* Paris, 1924, p. 86.

[2] Articles 3–22. The text consulted was the Arabic version found in *Wathāʾiq wa-Nuṣūṣ,* Cairo, 1955, vol. I.

[3] For the touchy relationship between the Constitution and positive law on the one hand and *sharīʿah* law on the other, see Nadav Safran, *Egypt in Search of Political Community,* Cambridge, Mass., 1961, chap. 8.

[4] Articles 23–25.

[5] Article 36.

islature was to be convened in an extraordinary session to approve or reject such decrees.[6] In short, the Constitution was intended to transform the state into a limited monarchy, secular in character and liberal in outlook. Although neither the Wafd nor the Nationalist Party was represented on the drafting committee, they seemed to be generally satisfied with its provisions.[7]

'Abd al-Khāliq Tharwat Pasha, the Premier and the guiding spirit behind the drafting committee, had pushed the scheme rapidly forward in the hope of having the Constitution promulgated during his premiership. However, King Fuad had been unhappy all along about the Constitution, which he regarded as detracting from his royal powers, and even tried unsuccessfully to have Tharwat's friend and former colleague 'Adli Pasha intercede to amend the draft in his favor.

When it became evident that Tharwat would not be deflected from his goal of having the Constitution issued without amendment, Fuad contrived his resignation through a series of rumors and threats of arranged demonstrations. A new ministry, ready to do Fuad's bidding, was installed. This ministry, headed by Nasīm Pasha, proceeded surreptitiously to amend several provisions which were said to detract from the King's power. The amendments, among other things, abolished the provision that the nation was the source of powers, equalized the number of senators appointed to those elected, empowered the King to issue decrees having the force of law even during a legislative session, and recognized the King's exclusive prerogatives in relation to Muslim institutions of learning and *waqfs* (instead of having the exercise of such prerogatives regulated by law).[8] However, this ministry resigned in February, 1923, after acceding to the British in deleting from the Constitution the provisions dealing with the Sudan, and another new ministry, headed by Yaḥya Ibrāhīm Pasha, came to power. By this time the amendments to

[6] Article 41.

[7] 'Abd al-Raḥman al-Rāfi'i, *Fi A'qāb al-Thawrah al-Miṣriyyah,* vol. I, Cairo, 1947–1951, p. 63.

[8] Al-Rāfi'i, *Fi A'qāb,* vol. I, pp. 72–74, 90.

the draft Constitution had become known to the public, and vehement protests were heard against them. The strongest protest came in the form of two open letters to the Prime Minister from 'Abd al-'Azīz Fahmi, a former president of the bar and member of the constitution-drafting committee. The letters gave both moral and legal arguments for adopting the original draft of the Constitution. Some of the provisions of the letters merit treatment not only because they had a great influence on public opinion, but because they demonstrate the extent to which liberal ideas had become part of the thinking of prominent lawyers in the country.[9]

Undoubtedly the gravest issue which engaged Fahmi's attention was the article stipulating that sovereignty emanated from the nation. He insisted that this article had been adopted by the committee after careful consideration and after "it had become apparent . . . that the authority of the nation is above every other authority." He characterized the proposed deletion as "turning things upside down whereby the Constitution . . . became a mere grant by the Crown, on the assumption that, fundamentally, the nation had no rights or authority or sovereignty." He urged that the Constitution be adopted in its original form, "not on the assumption that it is a mere gift, but that it is a firm right belonging to the nation and accruing in the form of an agreement between the nation—[as represented] by the ministers who are members of it—and His Majesty the King. i.e., in the nature of an offer by the Council of Ministers and an acceptance by the King." The social-contract ideas of government, negating absolutist pretensions, are immediately apparent in these remarks. The fact that it would take a long stretch of the imagination to think of the ministers as representing the people did not seem to bother Fahmi, who must have been carried away by his enthusiasm for democratic ideals.[10]

[9] The letters, one dated March 16 and the other April 15, 1923, are reproduced in al-Rāfi'i, *Fi A'qāb*, vol. I, pp. 100–112.

[10] The only justification for the idea of representation was the fact that when Tharwat Pasha agreed to form a government he "vol-

Another issue was the reported amendment empowering the King to dissolve not only the Chamber of Deputies, as originally planned, but also the Senate. Fahmi pointed out, quite rightly, that such a power over the Senate, which included senators appointed by the King, was a constant threat to them to fall into line.[11]

A similar issue was the attempt to make the appointment and dismissal of diplomatic representatives within the "special rights" of the King. Fahmi argued that in such a case "the ambassadors of Egypt abroad would become a toy in the hands of the Palace personnel . . . and the foreign policy of Egypt would become the policy of the Palace, not the policy of the Egyptian government." With regard to amendments such as the King's right to issue decrees and the confirmation of his privileges concerning institutions of religious education and *waqfs,* Fahmi was content to point out that these would entail great inherent dangers.

On April 19, 1923, four days after the second letter was published, the Constitution was issued in its unamended form, except for the provisions concerning the Sudan. The attendant circumstances, especially the fact that this action took place suddenly and at night, suggest that the Prime Minister must have been subjected to great pressure. The fact that his cabinet included three members of the drafting committee, including its vice-president, Aḥmad Ḥishmat Pasha, who was an uncle of Fahmi's, may have been a contributing factor.[12]

Although Fahmi's enthusiasm for the Constitution suffered a relapse when he joined the unconstitutional government of

unteered to represent the people" in drawing up the constitution. See al-Rāfiʿi, *Fi Aʿqāb,* vol. I, p. 111.

[11] When Saʿd Zaghlūl became Premier, he saw to it that the right of the King to appoint two-fifths of the membership of the Senate was exercised upon the recommendation of the cabinet. For the mediation of Baron Van Der Bosch, the attorney-general of the mixed courts, in this dispute, see al-Rāfiʿi, *Fi Aʿqāb,* vol. I, pp. 145–150.

[12] On Fahmi's relationship to Hishmat see ʿAbd al-ʿAzīz Fahmi, *Mudhakkirāt, al-Muṣawwar,* June 24, 1949.

Zīwar Pasha on March 13, 1925, it was quickly renewed after he was dismissed from office for his support of another liberal cause, that of 'Ali 'Abd al-Rāziq and his book *al-Islām wa-Uṣūl al-Ḥukm* (*Islam and the Fundamentals of Government*), which raised a furor in conservative circles. In a meeting held by the Liberal Constitutionalists on October 30, 1925, Fahmi expressed regret of his previous participation in the Zīwar government and called for the return to the Constitution and for free elections, a step on which the government procrastinated until May of the following year.

The Constitution suffered still another major upset. It was disregarded during the premiership of Muḥammad Maḥmūd and was completely abolished during the premiership of Ismā'īl Ṣidqi, who came to power on June 20, 1930. The high-handed manner in which Ṣidqi went about his rule, abolishing the Constitution on October 20 and substituting a much less liberal one, greatly aroused the lawyers, who considered themselves the upholders of constitutionality and the rule of law. No sooner had Ṣidqi taken this step than the general assembly of the bar was called to an extraordinary meeting to consider what could be done. The government intervened and forcibly prevented the meeting. Even the regular meeting of the general assembly held in December of each year was barred on the supposition that "the General Assembly might debate matters that could be considered political," as the chief clerk of the Cairo court of appeal, where the regular meetings of the bar were held, candidly put it in tendering to the president of the bar the decision to prevent the meeting.[13] The meeting was allowed to take place only when the president of the Court of Appeal was assured that no political topics would be discussed. These restrictive measures moved the lawyer-politician Muḥammad Ḥusayn Haykal to say that even "in the harshest days of British martial-law rule" the bar

[13] *Minutes of the National Bar Association*, part I, pp. 52–50; Muḥammad Ḥusayn Haykal et al., *al-Siyāsah al-Miṣriyyah*, Cairo, 1921, pp. 39–40.

was able to meet and publish its resolutions concerning the political situation.

It is ironic that these restrictive measures should have come at the hands of a Premier who had studied law under the liberal legal tradition of France and was thus well aware of the importance of basic constitutional guarantees and fundamental human rights. His autocratic actions were opposed by the great majority of political leaders in the country, particularly the leaders of the Wafd and the Liberal Constitutional Parties, many of whom were prominent lawyers. As a direct result of their pressure, the Constitution was restored in 1935.

Ṣidqi was destined to come into conflict again with the lawyers, this time as a result of the Bevin-Ṣidqi draft agreement to settle the issues outstanding between Egypt and Britain, particularly the evacuation of British troops from Egypt and the defense of the Middle East. Ṣidqi, who had formed his second cabinet in February, 1946, and had failed to arrive at an agreement with the British in the official negotiations which took place in Cairo, proceeded to London with Ibrāhīm ʻAbd al-Hādi, his Foreign Minister, and carried on negotiations directly with British Foreign Secretary Ernest Bevin. The resulting draft agreement[14] was opposed both by public opinion in Egypt and by seven of the twelve-member officially appointed negotiating delegation as not meeting national demands. In connection with this opposition and the demonstrations it evoked, some university students were put on trial for whipping up feelings conducive to violence, and lawyers who volunteered to defend them in court were arrested by the police without a warrant from the Attorney General's office, as was necessary in such circumstances. In the extraordinary meeting of the general assembly of the bar, held on November 29, 1946, to deal with the incident, the members attacked both the reported arrest of the advocates and the draft agreement with equal vigor. One member accused the gov-

[14] By the terms of the draft the British government agreed to complete the evacuation of Egypt by 1949; the Sudan was covered by a protocol which in effect postponed its consideration to a future date.

ernment of "holding onto a philosophy which belittles the people and despises law." Makram 'Ubayd suggested that the strike of advocates, which was being discussed as a retaliatory measure against the government, should be declared to be in support of "Egyptian freedom and professional, i.e., judicial, freedom. . . . We defend everybody's freedom, whether it be that of an individual, of a group or of people and country." A third member put the incident in its true context: "The country is in danger, and the first symptom of this danger is that the whip of the executioner has fallen upon the shoulders of the lawyers. But the executioner is not interested in the lawyers *per se;* he wants to strike the nation by hitting those who come forward to defend their country, so that those whom we defend will come to feel that [lawyers] have failed in their defense." A resolution passed unanimously at the meeting declared the Bevin-Ṣidqi draft agreement unacceptable and further called for a two-day strike to protest both the arrest of the advocates and the agreement.[15]

The lawyers' fight against martial law in the aftermath of the two occasions on which it was decreed—on May 13, 1948, in connection with the Arab-Israeli war, and on January 26, 1952, the day Cairo was sacked by mobs—was no less vehement. Although on both occasions the declaration of martial law was actually justified for the preservation of state security, the governments then in power used the arbitrary power accorded them under martial law as a means to curb or stifle any opposition. The hostilities in Palestine had been officially terminated by a truce signed by Egypt and Israel at Rhodes on February 24, 1949, but martial law was renewed anyway on May 15, 1949, for one more year. To be sure, the period before and after the Palestine war was characterized by several assassinations and attempted assassinations of persons in high places—on many occasions involving members of the fanatical Muslim Brotherhood—but most lawyers felt that such crimes could be

[15] *Minutes,* part II, pp. 403, 402. The uproar against the agreement, particularly its Sudan provisions, completely wrecked it.

adequately dealt with by the ordinary machinery of the courts. Accordingly, when the general assembly of the bar was called to an extraordinary meeting on October 14, 1949, to deal primarily with a proposal to hold a public celebration in connection with the termination of the mixed courts that day, as stipulated by the Treaty of Montreux, the occasion was seized upon by the members to voice their protests against the continuation of martial law and the detention of scores of people without trial. The fact that there were several lawyers among those detained seemed to add impetus to their protests and calls for action. The general assembly met again two weeks later, and for a third time on November 18, to deliberate on a possible course of action. When mere protests were found inadequate to sway the government, a resolution was passed approving in principle a strike by lawyers throughout the country.[16] The changes in government in that period appear to have put the decision in abeyance, but martial law was not lifted until May 1, 1950, after the Wafd Party had been returned to power.[17]

The burning and sacking of Cairo by mobs on January 26, 1952, following a period of constant skirmishing between Egyptian volunteer fighters and British forces in the vicinity of the Suez Canal, produced a declaration of martial law that very evening.[18] By May the restrictions on personal liberty were such that more than fifty lawyers petitioned the board of the bar for an extraordinary meeting of the general assembly to air their views on that dismal situation. What especially provoked them was a decree which made it *ultra vires* for the Council of State to entertain cases involving orders issued by the martial-law authorities, thus placing those orders beyond judicial review. When the assembly met on May 30, 1952, it unanimously

[16] *Minutes,* part II, pp. 279–271.

[17] For these developments see al-Rāfi'i, *Fi A'qāb,* vol. III, pp. 295–309.

[18] For a graphic description of the burning of Cairo, see Jean Lacouture and Simonne Lacouture, *Egypt in Transition,* London, 1958, pp. 105–122.

resolved that the continuance of martial law was without any justification and should cease immediately. It further resolved that the objectionable decree, which "bestows upon the actions of the military-law authorities an immunity which the letter and spirit of the Constitution do not condone," should be repealed.[19] Events moved rapidly, however, and before the assembly could meet again to take further action the army revolt of July 23, 1952, had instituted a military dictatorship under which action in behalf of a liberal and constitutional government, as understood in the West, became impossible.

The opposition to martial law and authoritarian rule was indicative of the concepts of liberty and personal freedom which had been propagated in Egypt for about a century. The mixed courts and bar associations had played a major role in this regard,[20] but equally important was the role of some individual Egyptian lawyers.

Among those responsible for the introduction of Western political thought and ideas of liberty and freedom were two lawyers, Fatḥi Zaghlūl (1863–1914), an older brother of Sa'd Zaghlūl, and Luṭfi al-Sayyid (1872–1962). Zaghlūl, who had studied law in France and occupied several judicial posts before becoming Undersecretary of Justice in 1907, felt that for progressive laws to be effective in a society the society itself must be a worthy subject of those laws. Accordingly, he devoted much of his time to translating Western books which seemed to him to embody the principles of freedom and altruistic thought.[21] As early as 1888 he began a translation of Rousseau's *Social Contract,* a task he never completed. Four years later he published his translation of Bentham's *Principles of Legislation* and

[19] *Minutes,* part II, pp. 185–184.

[20] See the discussion in Chapter Two.

[21] See Aḥmad Luṭfi al-Sayyid, Mudhakkirāt, *al-Muṣawwar,* November 3, 1950. These memoirs have recently appeared in book form under the title *Qiṣṣat Ḥayāti* (ed. by Ṭāhir Ṭanāḥi), but some of the original ideas have been tampered with to conform to the new philosophy of the state.

later translated, among other works, Edmond Demolin's *A quoi tient la superiorité des Anglo-Saxons* and Le Bon's *L'Esprit de la Societé.* Speaking of these translations, his friend and admirer Luṭfi al-Sayyid said:[22]

> In [translating] these books he had a definite goal . . . the propagation of the principles of freedom—the freedom of the individual and that of the nation. . . . He saw that the nation had been passing since 1882 [the 'Arābi revolt] through a series of contradictory phases . . . thus he wanted to present to the people Rousseau's *Social Contract* so that they would know the rights of the individual, the rights of the nation, and the authority the latter is entitled to. . . . Perhaps Fatḥi Pasha [Zughlūl] was afraid of the all-too-apparent tendency toward a quasi-socialism as it affected the freedom of individuals and the education of the nation, for people were no longer content with demanding their rights to freedom . . . but they started to demand that the government undertake to do everything for them. . . . Such a movement necessarily makes the government everything and the individual nothing. . . . Zaghlūl, therefore, started indirectly to guide individuals to the necessity of holding onto their personality and to demonstrate to them that personality training was the secret behind the precedence of the Anglo-Saxons. He demanded, as it were, that the Egyptians follow the example of the Anglo-Saxons lest their personality disappear, and with it their very existence.

In sizing up his friend, al-Sayyid said that Zaghlūl believed so strongly in the school of democracy—whether concerning education or social, political, and economic principles—and in the orderly evolution of society that he hated revolution in any of its aspects, even that of thought. Of Fatḥi Zaghlūl's own two books, *Commentary on the Civil Code* and *al-Muḥāmāh*

[22] Al-Sayyid, *al-Muṣawwar,* November 3, 1950.

(*Advocacy*), the latter made an important contribution to the proper understanding of the role of advocates in the defense of rights.[23]

Luṭfi al-Sayyid's own writings on liberty and freedom[24] had far greater popular influence because of his work in journalism and position as rector of the Egyptian University, a career which gained for him the epithet *ustādh al-jīl,* teacher of this generation. As editor of *al-Jarīdah,* the daily organ of the Ummah (Nation) Party, he was able to disseminate his views on many national issues, and as rector of the university (from 1924 to 1941, with two periods of interruption) he was in a position to mold public opinion. Most of al-Sayyid's writings on freedom appeared in the form of editorials in *al-Jarīdah* addressed to the deputies in the new Legislative Assembly, which was elected in 1913. Since the editorials dealt with issues before the assembly or soon to be taken up by it, his ideas must have been read and discussed widely at the time; the fact that these editorials were later published several times in book form[25] supports the assumption that al-Sayyid's ideas continued to influence later generations.

More than any other Egyptian writer, al-Sayyid came closest to the ideas of the nineteenth-century liberalism in his insistence on individualism and the limitation of the role of government to the maintenance of order, the administration of justice, and defense. He was thus concerned with both the safeguarding of personal rights and the noninterference of government in matters that should be left to private initiative. For example, he exhorted the assembly not to interfere with the rights of the public, which he enumerated as "(1) the right of personal freedom in its general sense: freedom of thought, of

[23] For Zaghlūl's obituary see *al-Hilāl,* vol. 22, May, 1914, p. 628.

[24] For a discussion of al-Sayyid's life and works see Safran, pp. 90–97; Jamal M. Aḥmad, *The Intellectual Origins of Egyptian Nationalism,* London, 1960; Albert H. Hourani, *Arabic Thought in the Liberal Age,* 1798–1939, London, 1962.

[25] For example, *Ta'ammulāt,* Cairo, 1946; *Mushkilat al-Ḥurriyyah,* Beirut, 1959.

belief, of speech and writing, and of education—all limited only by the noninfliction of harm on others . . . (2) the right of equality before the law . . . (3) the right of property which the legislator should not deprive an individual or a group of . . . and which forms an important pillar of society . . . [and] (4) the right of the nation . . . to be free."[26] He further insisted that government, whatever form it might take, has no reason to exist except necessity, and that its authority should not go beyond the requirements of that necessity. Accordingly, he characterized as tyrannical any but the liberal system of government (*madhhab al-ḥurriyyah*), and in this respect he made no distinction between monarchy, oligarchy, or socialist government, because all three, he felt, "would sacrifice the interests of the individual to the government or the group."[27]

In summing up his public activities al-Sayyid ascribed their mainspring to his commitment to freedom: "I sought for Egypt freedom, a constitution, unrestrained education, and inviolability of character because freedom is life, or rather it is dearer than life; it is to man's upward development what the soul is to the body."[28]

By the 1920s there was a widespread understanding of these concepts and ideals, especially among lawyers and government officials, whose jobs required them to think in terms of rights and duties, authority and immunity, sovereignty and personal freedom. The adoption of a democratic constitution in 1923 was a logical result. Even though democracy was at that time facing considerable difficulties in Europe, the Egyptian jurist 'Abd al-Razzāq al-Sanhūri publicly defended it as the best system of government yet devised by man.[29]

[26] Aḥmad Luṭfi al-Sayyid, *al-Muntakhabāt,* vol. II, Cairo, 1945, pp. 72–74.

[27] Al-Sayyid, *al-Muntakhabāt,* vol. II, pp. 65, 92.

[28] Aḥmad Luṭfi al-Sayyid, Mudhakkirāt, *al-Muṣawwar,* August 31, 1950.

[29] Al-Ta'bīr 'an Ra'y al-Ummah, *al-Hilāl,* vol. 46, April, 1938, pp. 601–603.

The liberal attitudes of the Western-oriented lawyers were perhaps most evident in the area of politics. This liberality, a modal point to which they approximated in varying degrees, can be attributed to the natural preference of the legal profession for moderate and orderly change, to its mistrust of dictatorship and individual authority, and to the independence and moral courage of individual lawyers in championing unpopular causes.

In 1907 Muṣṭafa Kāmil was meeting with great success in attracting people to his Nationalist Party, especially after the Denshiway incident had aroused the Egyptian public. However, some prominent lawyers who had looked askance at the Nationalist Party's radical approach joined with a number of notables to form the Ummah (Nation) Party to work for the goal of independence by more moderate means. Among this group were Fatḥi Zaghlūl, the president of the Cairo court of first instance and member of the Denshiway trials court; Luṭfi al-Sayyid, who became secretary-general of the party and editor of its newspaper *al-Jarīdah;* Qāsim Amīn, a judge and famous advocate of the rights of women; Aḥmad 'Afifi, a judge in the court of appeal; 'Abd al-'Azīz Fahmi, a prominent advocate; and 'Abd al-Khāliq Tharwat, then an outstanding official in the Ministry of Justice. The fact that several members of the Ummah Party were officials in an administration dominated by the British made the party open to the accusation that it was "in touch with the British government," a charge which al-Sayyid implicitly denied.[30]

The men who made up the Ummah Party all believed in varying degrees in a rational approach to the question of independence, with emphasis upon a solid foundation, in contrast to the Nationalist Party's tumultuous and intransigent demands for immediate and complete British evacuation. Their attitude can best be exemplified by al-Sayyid's statement to Khedive

[30] Al-Sayyid, Mudhakkirāt, *al-Muṣawwar,* September 7, 1950. For the moderate nature of the party see Fahmi, Mudhakkirāt, *al-Muṣawwar,* December 2, 1949.

'Abbās in 1898, after a trip to Switzerland in search of support for the independence of Egypt: "Egypt cannot attain its independence except through the efforts of its sons; national interest demands that H.E. the Khedive lead an extensive movement for public education."[31] It is not surprising, therefore, that the intellectual members of the Ummah Party were in the lead of those Egyptians who in 1908 successfully realized through general subscription the creation of the Egyptian University.[32]

The attitude of 'Abd al-Khāliq Tharwat Pasha was an outstanding example of moderate liberalism in the attainment of national goals. Tharwat first enunciated his views in a speech as chief prosecutor in the trial of Wirdāni, the assassin of Prime Minister Buṭrus Pasha Ghāli, in 1910:[33]

> We are foremost among those who highly esteem concern with public questions and who consider it a duty laid upon every Egyptian to strive by legal means for the progress of the country and its people. . . . Likewise it is our opinion that among the factors conducive to the progress of nations is criticism of the actions of those in authority. But we cannot concede that a person attain the position of government critic unless he has, in addition to great knowledge and profound wisdom, a faculty of level-headedness in word and deed, so that he might rightly evaluate actions, discern matters with sound thought, and not overstep the bounds of legality. Otherwise, [public] service becomes a curse and the will for good becomes an evil.

Tharwat thus set high store in working for the general progress of the country through legal means rather than by force, revolution, or anarchy. This belief led him to a diplomatic

[31] Al-Sayyid, Mudhakkirāt, *al-Muṣawwar,* September 7, 1950.

[32] For the faith of the Egyptians in education as the overriding force for bringing about democratic government see Safran, p. 148.

[33] Muḥammad Ḥusayn Haykal, *Tarājim Miṣriyyah wa-Gharbiyyah,* Cairo, n.d., pp. 194–195.

approach seldom followed by other Egyptian politicians. His success in eliciting the Declaration of February 28, 1922, on the independence of Egypt was perhaps a direct result of his avowed policy of negotiating "not by publicly declaring his demands and striving for their attainment by force, intrigue, or bargaining, but by formulating his aims to himself and by depending above all on discussions which were coupled with wisdom, logic, and the dictates of reason."[34] In the aftermath of that declaration he consistently called for the strict observance of law and order, and in reference to the reservations and guarantees insisted upon by the British in connection with the granting of independence, he publicly stated: "The main argument [of the British] in their desire for guarantees is their extreme wariness concerning their interests . . . and their lack of confidence in entrusting them to our care. If we, therefore, should put an end to all elements of disturbance and strife . . . we would effectively answer that argument.[35]

Another important figure who pursued this course of moderation and rationality in politics was Muḥammad Ḥusayn Haykal. In 1918 Haykal and a group of youthful liberal friends had organized a Democratic Party in order to seek representation in the *wafd* that was to plead the cause of Egypt at the Paris Peace Conference. When the country split into two camps as a result of the quarrel between ʿAdli Pasha and Saʿd Zaghlūl over the conduct of negotiations with the British government, Haykal found himself on the side of ʿAdli Pasha. When ʿAdli organized the Liberal Constitutionalist Party Haykal was selected as editor of the party's newspaper, *al-Siyāsah,* first published on October 30, 1922. Thus Haykal left the practice of law for politics and journalism.

In this period, and especially after Saʿd Zaghlūl had been exiled to the Seychelles by the British authorities, the split between the two factions deepened, and "the battle between Saʿd and his enemies was no longer a battle between politicians

[34] Haykal, *Tarājim,* p. 202.
[35] Haykal, *Tarājim,* p. 208.

who were fencing with arguments and logic, but a battle between a prophet whom Heaven had sent . . . and dissidents whose national treason had reached the bounds of infidelity."[36] Accordingly, no sooner had *al-Siyāsah* started publishing than accusations of national treason were leveled against it. In fact, nineteen days after its first issue two members of the Liberal Constitutionalist Party were assassinated as they were leaving its headquarters, although the intended victim had been Premier Tharwat Pasha.[37] However, the editor and owners of *al-Siyāsah* refused to be intimidated. Most of them had been educated in Europe and believed "that knowledge was the thing which prescribed the course of the world, that reason should have the upper hand, and that the frivolous playing with [peoples'] minds could not conquer reason or subdue its radiant light."[38] When Sa'd Zaghlūl became Prime Minister, charges of contempt of parliament were leveled against Haykal for a series of articles attacking "the party of 600," those members of the parliament who had demanded an increase in yearly remuneration to £ E600. In a later article entitled Come, Supporters of Freedom, Repel the Attack on Freedom, he urged every Egyptian who valued freedom to stand up to demonstrators, who were attacking people and throwing bricks at homes. When the public prosecutor construed this article as an attempt to overthrow the government and ordered subsequent issues of *al-Siyāsah* confiscated, the Egyptian courts would not sanction such an action; this moved Haykal to declare in a later article: "In truth there *are* judges in Egypt. As long as law has its upholders, the people should be reassured and should take refuge in the judiciary whenever injustice or tyranny befall them."[39]

This resistance to the monolithic and charismatic tendencies of Sa'd Zaghlūl had also been shared by 'Abd al-'Azīz Fahmi,

[36] Aḥmad Luṭfi al-Sayyid (ed.), *al-Duktūr Muḥammad Ḥusayn Haykal,* Cairo, 1958, p. 23.

[37] See the discussion in Chapter Four.

[38] Al-Sayyid, *al-Duktūr Haykal,* p. 24.

[39] Al-Sayyid, *al-Duktūr Haykal,* p. 28.

a prominent member of the Egyptian *wafd* to Paris and London in 1919. Not only had Fahmi opposed entrusting the chairmanship of the *wafd* to Zaghlūl "for reasons which good form prevents me from divulging," but he resigned from that body in protest against two telegrams sent from Europe to the Egyptian newspaper *al-Akhbār,* one with the connivance of Zaghlūl and the other by Zaghlūl personally, attacking the statesman 'Adli Pasha and "those who want to enter into negotiations [with the British] without compliance with the reservations made by the nation."[40]

Fahmi's independence and moral courage were reflected not only in politics, but also in the fields of legal practice and government administration, where his insistence on the protection of rights won him great esteem in legal circles. As a practicing lawyer he made the representatives of Sultan Ḥusayn Kāmil apologize to him in the daily newspapers for a critical remark passed among a group of lawyers concerning Fahmi's defense of a government employee accused of embezzlement. As Minister of Justice in the second Zīwar government, which took office March 13, 1925, Fahmi consistently avoided an amendment to the Penal Code—just as consistently demanded by King Fuad—which would have placed the Palace personnel in a privileged position in connection with criticism by the daily press.[41] His famous two open letters against the amendments to the Constitution typified his general stand.

Fahmi's profound liberal spirit is best illustrated by his defense of freedom of opinion in the case of Shaykh 'Ali 'Abd al-Rāziq. In 1925, when Fahmi was Minister of Justice, suit was brought before the supreme council of al-Azhar to deprive 'Abd al-Rāziq, who was at that time a *sharī'ah* judge, of his *'ālimiyyah* and the privileges pertaining to it, including the qualification to hold a *sharī'ah* judgeship, for having written the

[40] Fahmi, Mudhakkirāt, *al-Muṣawwar,* December 2, December 9, 1949.

[41] Fahmi, Mudhakkirāt, *al-Muṣawwar,* June 24, December 23, 1949.

book *al-Islām wa-Uṣūl al-Ḥukm* (*Islam and the Fundamentals of Government*) in which he attempted to establish that the caliphate was not an integral part of Islam and therefore should be abolished.[42] The case aroused great interest, and 'Abd al-Rāziq was bitterly attacked by the orthodox groups. Fahmi, undaunted by the violent condemnation of the book and its writer, attempted to find a means of defending 'Abd al-Rāziq. When he failed he resigned his ministerial position. In Fahmi's words:[43]

> I read the book once and twice but could find not the least idea that would subject the author to censure. . . . And since the case was predicated upon the charge that Shaykh 'Ali had violated the code of the *'ālimiyyah* degree, I asked ['Abd al-Khāliq] Tharwat Pasha and [Isma'īl] Ṣidqi Pasha—two of those who had worked on the basic law of al-Azhar—whether the intention was to prescribe a punishment for the [expression] of opinion, a thing which would be contrary to every rule of law. They answered that that had never passed through their minds. Whereupon I turned towards the source of this case and argued with the secretary-general of the Supreme Council [of al-Azhar] that the Council had no jurisdiction in the matter. . . . But, unfortunately, Shaykh 'Ali was deprived of the *'alimiyyah* degree.
>
> Yaḥya Ibrāhīm Pasha, who was then acting Premier due to the absence of Zīwar Pasha, who was then on vacation, forwarded to me a copy of the judgment that had been sent by the rectorate of al-Azhar to the Premier's office and asked me to enforce it. The enforcement meant, naturally, that I instruct the personnel office to remove Shaykh 'Ali from the cadre of *sharī'ah* judges.

[42] For an account of this book see Charles Clarence Adams, *Islam and Modernism in Egypt*, London, 1933, pp. 261–268.

[43] Fahmi, Mudhakkirāt, *al-Muṣawwar*, December 23, 1949. For the support which Haykal gave to Shaykh 'Ali 'Abd al-Rāziq see Haykal's article in al-Sayyid, *al-Duktūr Haykal*, p. 69.

The enforcement of this judgment which was void *per se* . . . weighed heavily on my conscience. . . . I felt duty bound, in fairness to my conscience and to the public interest, to transmit the judgment to the chief legal men in the government, namely the counselors of the committee on [government] cases, and to ask them about the efficacy of the judgment and whether the Ministry of Justice was bound to enforce it. When Yaḥya Ibrāhīm Pasha learned of my action he became angry and said to me, "It looks as if we are not in agreement in our work; if one does not want to work with us, let him resign." I answered, ". . . You know that I often expressed my desire to resign, but now I shall not do so, for in this particular judgment I am defending a right in which I believe" . . . whereupon Yaḥya Pasha adopted a very easy stratagem; instead of dismissing me from the Ministry of Justice he issued a decree transferring my duties to the Minister of Education. . . . So I stayed away from my office. . . . [My colleagues] Muḥammad 'Ali 'Allūbah Pasha and Tawfīq Dūs Pasha expressed their solidarity with me by resigning, and so did Ismā'īl Ṣidqi Pasha, who was then in Europe."

Luṭfi al-Sayyid took a similar stand in the case of Ṭāha Ḥusayn, a well-known literary figure. In 1926, when al-Sayyid was rector of the Egyptian University, Ḥusayn, who was a teacher there, published a book entitled *Fi al-Shi'r al-Jāhili* (*On Pre-Islamic Poetry*) in which he cast strong doubts on the authenticity of the pre-Islamic poetry that had been used throughout the Islamic period by grammarians and exegetes to explain the Koran and demonstrate its rhetorical elegance. No sooner had the book appeared than a storm of protest arose, and accusations of an intent to undermine the Muslim religion were hurled at the writer. Al-Sayyid, who had become the chief advocate of liberty and free speech through his articles in *al-Jarīdah,* stood firmly by him and would not accept his resignation from the university when it was offered. To be sure, the book was suppressed, and Ḥusayn had to stand trial on charges, instituted by the rector of al-Azhar and others, of attacking the state religion. The charges were dismissed, and it was thought that if Ḥusayn were to leave the country for a year things would simmer down. However, in 1932, during the premiership of Ismā'īl Ṣidqi Pasha, the issue was resurrected, and in March of that year the Ministry of Education transferred Ḥusayn from his position as dean of the faculty of arts to some post in the ministry without consulting the university. Although in point of law the ministry was entitled to do this, al-Sayyid considered the move an interference with the independence and integrity of the university. He met with the Premier and demanded that Ḥusayn be returned to the university at least as a professor, if not as a dean, but the Council of Ministers turned him down. The only honorable course al-Sayyid felt open to him was to resign. When he was approached in 1935 to take up the rectorate again, he demanded, and obtained, a change in the basic law of the university that would make the transfer of a professor to a position outside it dependent upon the consent of the university senate.[44]

The strong conservatism of the orthodox elements illustrated in both these cases gives some indication of the rigidity of the social establishment, and hence the extent to which lawyers were prepared to go in defending the right of free speech and freedom of opinion.

Greater freedom for women was another area in which liberal lawyers were instrumental in effecting reforms. Foremost in this area was Qāsim Amīn, who had studied law in France and joined the judiciary upon his return to Egypt in 1885. Amīn had been profoundly influenced by French liberal thought and was deeply concerned about the great chasm which separated the Egyptian woman from her European sister. His two books, *Taḥrīr al-Mar'ah* (*The Emancipation of Women*), and *al-Mar'ah*

[44] Al-Sayyid, Mudhakkirāt, *al-Muṣawwar*, November 17, 1950; Adams, p. 255.

al-Jadīdah (*The New Woman*), which appeared in 1899 and 1901, respectively, had great influence upon the social and legal amelioration in the position of Egyptian women, despite the fact that some of his ideas might seem conservative by modern standards.[45]

Amīn started his campaign in full expectation of attack by the traditional forces; what surprised him, however, was the bitter opposition from Muṣṭafa Kāmil, Khedive ʻAbbās, and other modernist leaders. This opposition may have stemmed from the desire of Kāmil and ʻAbbās to humor and placate the populace, who held dearly to their customs and superstitions, for political purposes.[46] Be that as it may, Kāmil's chief interest was in the propagation of a deep faith in Egypt and devotion to its independence, and he evidently lacked a philosophy of freedom or social reform that would have made him side with Amīn. The opposition of Kāmil and his newspaper *al-Liwāʼ* was offset, however, by the support from Luṭfi al-Sayyid, his followers and associates, and their press organ *al-Jarīdah.* The most enthusiastic of the group was Haykal.[47] The progress achieved by women in Egypt during the past half century is undoubtedly a direct reflection of these early activities.

[45] For Qāsim Amīn's espousal of freedom of opinion, see Haykal, *Tarājim,* p. 154.

[46] Haykal, *Tarājim,* pp. 142–143.

[47] Al-Sayyid, *al-Duktūr Haykal,* p. 14.

CHAPTER SIX

lawyers and legal reform

The interest of lawyers in legal reform was a logical outgrowth of their professional involvement. This interest embraced both those technical aspects of law that might be described as "lawyers' law," which generated concern almost exclusively in legal circles, and those aspects which had a broader base of public involvement and even gave rise to public debate. It is these latter aspects that best exemplify the interaction of Egyptian lawyers with society. The issues which raised enough heated discussions, arguments, and counterarguments to classify as public debate related in the main to the unification of the judicial system, the reform of those aspects of the *sharī'ah* that were still being applied by the courts—especially the law of personal status—and the extent to which the *sharī'ah* was to form part of a new civil code or even of all codes. What interests us here is not the reform itself so much as the reasons for it, the attitudes of lawyers to it, and the significance of the change in their eyes.[1]

COURT REFORM

The creation of the mixed and the national courts in the late 1800s went a long way toward correcting the chaos in the courts,[2] but the situation was still far from satisfactory because of the multiplicity and uncertainty of jurisdiction and the resultant delay in justice. During the 1800s Egypt had been intent upon emulating Europe and had been ready to accord legal privileges to its citizens. In the early 1900s, however, the country was swept by a spirit of nationalism which gave precedence to all things national and was aimed at consolidating the basic fabric of the nation. The first institution subjected to this unifying movement was the mixed courts. Since these courts had originated in the capitulations and the customary practices grafted upon them, it was natural that the nationalist movement, which was out to abolish the capitulations altogether, also directed its attention to the mixed courts and their gradual elimination.

The popular literature protesting the continued functioning of the mixed courts is immense, and a well-reasoned article by the famous Egyptian jurist 'Abd al-Ḥamīd Badawi, who in 1946 became a member of the International Court of Justice at The Hague, sums up the major Egyptian complaints against those courts.[3] It is significant that Badawi did not attribute any cor-

[1] For the many aspects of reform see James Norman Dalrymple Anderson, *Islamic Law in the Modern World*, New York, 1959, and his series of nine articles, Recent Developments in Sharī'a Law, *The Muslim World*, vols. 40–42, 1950–1952. See also Joseph Schacht, *An Introduction to Islamic Law*, London, 1964, pp. 100–111; N. J. Coulson, *A History of Islamic Law*, Edinburgh, 1964, pp. 149–225.

[2] See the discussion in Chapter Two.

[3] The article, written in 1933 on the occasion of the fiftieth anniversary of the founding of the national courts, is 'Abd al-Ḥamīd Badawi, Athar al-Imtiyāzat fi al-Qaḍā' wa-al-Tashrī' fi Miṣr, in *al-Kitāb al-Dhahabi lil-Maḥākim al-Ahliyyah*, vol. II, Cairo, 1938, pp. 1–61. An-

ruption or incompetence to the mixed courts.[4] The two basic charges were, rather, that the mixed courts were trespassing upon the national sovereignty of Egypt by their ever-expanding jurisdiction, and that they were overzealous in the protection of foreign interests.

On the first score Badawi even rapped Nubar Pasha, the moving spirit of the mixed courts, for consenting to place under their jurisdiction matters which had been usurped by the various consular tribunals and which had never formed a part of the capitulations. He complained that for the sixty-odd years the mixed courts had existed their basic law had been only superficially amended, despite the repeated Egyptian requests for change, and despite the fact that Egypt had advanced to a degree that would entitle it to retrieve those rights which it had voluntarily abandoned. His greatest grievance was the fact that the mixed courts had enlarged their jurisdiction through a doctrine called "the doctrine of mixed interest," under which they assumed jurisdiction even in cases between Egyptians if such cases touched upon "foreign" interests, regardless of whether the owners of those interests intervened in the cases or were served with process. This doctrine, according to Badawi, extended to purely Egyptian corporations if one of the shareholders was a "foreigner," or even if a "foreigner" could obtain their shares, a situation that prompted Egyptian corporations to prohibit the sale of their shares to non-Egyptians in order to escape the jurisdiction of the mixed courts. In addition, the attempt by the mixed courts to acquire jurisdiction over all foreigners in Egypt, including those who were not even citizens of the capitulatory powers, and the attempt to arrogate to themselves jurisdiction over cases of maintenance and the constitution of *waqfs* which

---

other Egyptian jurist who was very active against the mixed courts, although he served in them as a counselor, was 'Abd al-Salām Dhihni.

[4] A prominent Egyptian lawyer, Muḥammad Kāmil Malash, who had been a judge with the mixed courts, even spoke nostalgically about the high standards and prestige of those courts. Interview in February, 1958.

had been intended to be within the jurisdiction of the personal-status courts, alarmed Badawi and the entire nation against this ever-expanding organism.[5]

In addition to this mixed-interest doctrine, Badawi declared that the overzealousness of the mixed courts in protecting foreigners led them to support foreigners' claims of exemption from taxation and to fail even to enforce police regulations touching upon foreigners if such regulations had not been assented to by the powers concerned. These jealously guarded privileges prompted Badawi to declare that the mixed courts "permitted the foreigners to live at the margin of the [Egyptian] nation, enjoying all the facilities and means of liberty, comfort, and affluence without shouldering more than the very least of costs and responsibilities—and all this at a time when the various powers were doubling the responsibilities and limitations imposed upon their own citizens, so much so that advanced nations, without an exception, were now complaining of the tyranny of the state over liberties and private interests."[6]

Badawi's attack on the mixed courts had been preceded by another attack by Egypt's foremost jurist, 'Abd al-'Azīz Fahmi. In his capacity as president of the bar association Fahmi had vehemently opposed the British plan put forward by Sir William E. Brunyate, the Judicial Adviser from 1916 to 1918, to substitute Britain for the other capitulatory powers in the exercise of their privileges. In 1933, speaking as president of the National Court of Cassation at the fiftieth-anniversary celebration of the founding of the national courts, Fahmi again called for abolishing the mixed courts. Addressing King Fuad from the rostrum, he said:[7]

[5] Badawi, pp. 16, 21, 25–27, 32–40.

[6] Badawi, pp. 41, 43, 53. Law 17 for the year 1911 attempted to solve the latter question by empowering the general assembly of the mixed court of appeal to pass on all additions and amendments to the mixed codes.

[7] Quoted in Badawi, p. 61. For a discussion of Fahmi's stand against the mixed courts see his obituary by 'Abd al-Razzāq al-Sanhūri in *Majallat Majlis al-Dawlah*, vol. II, January, 1951, pp. i–xi.

> We, the judges of the national courts, have been accustomed to hear from Your Majesty on every occasion certain reassuring words like "go forth with the blessings of God and his guidance, and be sure that your good actions will be rewarded . . . and that God is with the patient ones"—beautiful words carrying the utmost of encouragement—but it is time to crave that You raise your voice declaring that . . . Egypt has become worthy of . . . being independent in the administration of justice in its lands and for its entire inhabitants.

The agitation against the capitulations in general and the mixed courts in particular, and the increasing evidence of the ability of the national courts to deal with all judicial matters, resulted in 1937 in the Treaty of Montreux, which ended capitulations in Egypt and stipulated that the mixed courts were to continue only for a transitional period of twelve more years, after which time they were to be abolished and their jurisdiction transferred to the national courts. Thus on October 15, 1949, an institution that had contributed a major share to the legal development of Egypt passed from the scene.

The mixed courts were not the only judicial institution enjoying an independent and separate status that eventually had to succumb to the pressure of unification. The same lot fell to the *sharī'ah* courts and the various *millah,* or denominational, courts for the personal-status cases of Muslims and non-Muslims, respectively.[8] The *sharī'ah* courts, which had been the courts of general jurisdiction throughout the Islamic period, were reorganized in 1897 and again in 1931, thereby becoming an instrument of secular law instead of being based upon the authority of the *sharī'ah.* Their jurisdiction was limited to matters of personal status, including the constitution of *waqfs.* Since the law they applied was, with some modifications, the *sharī'ah* accord-

[8] For a summary of the constitution and jurisdiction of these courts see Shafīq Shiḥātah, *Tārīkh Ḥarakat al-Tajdīd fi al-Nuzum al-Qānūniyyah fi Miṣr,* pp. 71–84.

ing to the Ḥanafi school, and since they had a separate cadre, with qualifications different from those of the national courts, their separate status was maintained despite the fact that they could be regulated by law.

The *millah* courts traced their origin to the principle of the personality of the law, recognized by the Islamic empires, and were officially reaffirmed by the Ottoman Empire in the Hatti Humāyūn (Imperial Rescript) of 1856. By the beginning of the twentieth century these courts represented fourteen different Christian and Jewish denominations, each with its special council, or court, composed of clerics and prominent members of the denomination. These courts were even more independent than the *sharīʿah* courts in that they did not fall under the jurisdiction of the Minister of Justice and were not subject to regulation by secular law. The laws they applied were traditional, in some cases couched in the form of codes. Despite their greater independence, the jurisdiction of the *millah* courts fell far short of that of the *sharīʿah* courts; just before their abolishment in 1955 it was limited to marriage, divorce, and related personal and financial matters, whereas the jurisdiction of the *sharīʿah* courts embraced also testate and intestate succession and the constitution of *waqfs*. There was the further limitation that the parties to the dispute had to be of the same denomination; otherwise the *sharīʿah* courts, which were considered the courts of general jurisdiction for matters of personal status, had jurisdiction.[9]

Closely allied in function to the courts of personal status were the *ḥisbiyyah* councils, or courts of wards. These courts, which were separated from the *sharīʿah* courts in 1873 and reorganized in 1896, had judicial and administrative jurisdiction over the property of Muslim absent persons, minors, the insane, and others not of full legal capacity. In 1925 this jurisdiction was increased to cover the property of all such Egyptians or citizens of any country other than the capitulatory powers.[10] This step represented the first instance in which an Egyptian court was

[9] Shiḥātah, pp. 82–84.
[10] Shiḥātah, p. 79.

vested with general jurisdiction over all Egyptians in a matter of personal status and was an indication of more consolidation to come in that field.[11] The *ḥisbiyyah* councils were merged with the national courts in 1947, some eight years before the other personal-status courts met a similar fate.

Voices were raised far and wide in condemnation of the multiplicity of jurisdiction and legal entanglements. The arguments of these critics fell into three main categories: (1) that the purposes of the law were being defeated by legal trickery and the consequent escape from one jurisdiction to another, (2) that the constant conflict of jurisdiction between one system of courts and another was not only wasteful, but was also, because of delays, tantamount to a denial of justice, and (3) that in a nationalist and sovereign state there can be no room for separate jurisdictions based upon real or imagined privileges.

There is no doubt that the judicial process in the courts of special jurisdiction verged on total chaos. The *ḥisbiyyah* councils, for example, although they represent a great advance over the previous situation, drew the ire of lawyers because of the influence peddling of their lay members. In 1939 a prominent Cairo lawyer, revealing that a thick file of complaints against these courts was lodged in the Ministry of Justice pending investigation, called for their abolishment and for the transfer of their function to the national courts. He brushed aside arguments justifying their continuation—that they had been created to safeguard the secrets, dignity, and sensibilities of families whose members might become their wards—with the statement that the national courts, which were entrusted with the administration of penal law, surely could be trusted to deal with matters such as guardianship over minors and absent persons and interdiction.[12]

[11] Richard Debs, The Law of Property in Egypt, unpublished doctoral dissertation, Princeton University, Department of Oriental Studies, Princeton, N.J., 1963, p. 134.

[12] Farīd Anṭūn, *Mustaqbal al-Qaḍā' fi Miṣr*, Cairo, 1929, pp. 9–10. A similar proposal to consolidate the *ḥisbiyyah* and national

The evils of influence peddling in the *ḥisbiyyah* courts were far outdone by the legal trickery at the *millah* and *sharīʿah* courts and, before their abolishment, the mixed courts. The varieties of such chicanery were endless:

1. A non-Muslim woman sued her husband before a *millah* court for maintenance and obtained a judgment. The husband, in order to defeat that judgment, agreed with his mother that she sue him for maintenance before the *sharīʿah* court (which could have jurisdiction if both parties to a dispute agreed). A consent judgment for a large sum was entered, putting the mother in competition with the wife for that part of the man's income which could be legally attached.
2. A Catholic husband, who could not divorce his wife according to his personal-status law, turned Muslim and divorced her in accordance with the easy procedure provided by Muslim law, thus escaping the obligations he had assumed under his original faith.
3. A Greek Orthodox woman died, leaving a husband and minor sons and daughters. The husband was badly in debt, and not wishing to give his creditors recourse to any monies he might obtain as an heir, decided not to seek a share in the estate. The *millah* court divided the estate equally among the sons and daughters, and the husband was excluded according to the Byzantine law of that court. Several years later one of the sons reached majority and applied to the *sharīʿah* court for a redistribution of the estate according to Muslim law, whereby a son receives double the share of a daughter. At this point, now that the creditors had already settled for a fraction of the monies due to them, the husband stepped forward for his share according to Muslim law, claiming that he had never consented to the jurisdiction

courts was first made by Fatḥi Zaghlūl in 1913, but World War I intervened, and the proposal was forgotten.

of the *millah* court as provided by law for cases of inheritance. The national or mixed courts then had to decide how to untangle the knot.[13]

4. A Copt turned Muslim in order to divorce his wife, and his father died while he was "Muslim." Fearing exclusion from his father's estate because of the difference in religion, he applied to the Coptic *millah* court for reconversion to Christianity and a share in his father's estate, a request which was granted in the form of a judgment. Subsequently he became indebted for a large sum of money, and in order to defraud his creditors by putting his share of the estate outside their reach, he instigated his brother to bring suit in the *sharī'ah* court on the basis that the brother was in fact the sole heir because the first brother had been a Muslim at the time of the father's death, and Muslim law considers difference in religion between the *de cujus* and the presumptive heir as a bar to inheritance. Judgment to this effect was granted. The whole issue was then removed to the Court of Cassation to determine which of the two judgments was to be honored.[14]

These actual cases and hundreds like them cried out for redress. Prominent lawyers and jurists publicized them in order to move the government to action, and all wanted either an immediate or a gradual transfer of the jurisdiction of the personal-status courts to the national courts. Ḥāmid Zaki declared in this connection: "If we compare the National Courts . . . with the personal-status courts, we find that the former possess better guarantees for the realization of justice among litigants; proceedings before them are completely organized, and their

[13] These three examples are drawn from Aḥmad Ṣafwat, *Qaḍā' al-Aḥwāl al-Shakhṣiyyah lil-Ṭawā'if al-Milliyyah,* Cairo, 1936, pp. 40–45.

[14] Anṭūn, pp. 17–18. There is no record of the actual determination of this case.

judges are technical men who have specialized in disputes among people."[15]

The second group of arguments against the personal-status courts revolved around the fact that the conflict of jurisdiction among the various courts not only delayed justice, but because of the religious character of the courts, threatened to cause a religious conflict, a situation which had to be avoided if the country were to develop along national rather than religious lines. The possibilities of conflict were manifold. When the *ḥisbiyyah* courts were created there were immediate misgivings in the *sharīʿah* courts, and *sharīʿah* judges clamored for the return of their "usurped jurisdiction." Later, when the jurisdiction of the *ḥisbiyyah* courts was extended to non-Muslims, there was concern in the *millah* courts. The national courts also came into conflict with the *sharīʿah* courts, although *sharīʿah* jurisdiction, defined in the 1880 law which reorganized them and in subsequent amendments to that law, supposedly was to be restricted to "matters of personal status." However, since there was no general law for personal status, opinions differed in the courts as to what "matters of personal status" were or were not to include. The *sharīʿah* itself was no help in this regard, since it does not contain this term or the concomitant categorization. Nor did personal-status provisions introduced in laws of the mixed courts shed any light on this matter. Since each system of courts was intent upon expanding its own jurisdiction, clearly the only real solution was the unification of the entire court system.

The jurisdictional conflict between the *sharīʿah* and the *millah* courts assumed major proportions. It was in these courts that legal trickery was most rife, and it was to this conflict that the reforming lawyers paid particular attention. Three situations contributed to this conflict: (1) the overlapping jurisdiction of

[15] In addition to the works of Anṭūn and Ṣafwat, see, for example, Naṣīf Zaki, Masāʾil al-Aḥwāl al-Shakhṣīyyah, *al-Muḥāmāh,* vol. 20, 1940, pp. 1268–1290; Ḥāmid Zaki, al-Maḥākim al-Ahliyyah wa-al-Aḥwāl al-Shakhṣiyyah, *Majallat al-Qānūn wa-al-Iqtiṣād,* vol. 4, 1934, pp. 787–832.

both courts, (2) a change in denomination, or *millah,* by one of the spouses, and (3) the acceptance of Islam by one spouse.[16]

The first situation stemmed from the fact that the *sharī'ah* courts were considered the courts of general jurisdiction for personal status in Egypt. Accordingly, they had jurisdiction not only over Muslims, but also over all other persons, Egyptian or foreign, who either had no special court or did not signify their acceptance of *millah* jurisdiction. The majority of cases in this category were those in which a non-Muslim husband obtained a judgment against his wife from the *sharī'ah* court for return to the conjugal home and she obtained a judgment against him from a *millah* court for maintenance, or the reverse of this situation, where the wife sued for maintenance before the *sharī'ah* court and the husband sued for conjugal rights before the *millah* court. Often wives chose to sue before the *sharī'ah* court because it had the power to imprison the husband for nonpayment of maintenance, whereas *millah* courts had no such power.

The second situation was related in that the *sharī'ah* court, as the court of general jurisdiction, assumed jurisdiction in case of a difference in denomination of the spouses. However, when one spouse changed denomination after marriage, although the *sharī'ah* court claimed jurisdiction, the *millah* court also claimed it on the ground that the original marriage contract had been concluded under its laws and that it was the only body competent to administer those laws.

The third situation was similar, for when a non-Muslim husband accepted Islam, the *sharī'ah* court claimed jurisdiction over the marriage and the *millah* court also insisted on jurisdiction, as the "court of the marriage."[17]

Needless to say, in most cases the change in denomination or religion was effected not because of a change in belief, but because of the desire to avoid obligations assumed under the laws of the original denomination or religion. This dismal situa-

[16] For a general discussion of this conflict see Ṣafwat, *Qaḍā',* pp. 40–45.

[17] Ṣafwat, *Qaḍā',* pp. 40–45.

tion aroused the public-spirited lawyers, who perceived its dangers to morality and the rule of law. Farīd Anṭūn, for instance, declared:[18]

> What concerns us in these trying situations is not . . . [merely] the loss of time and money. The problem is much more grave because it is involved with morality and the social order itself, and because it leads to innumerable evils and sins. What evil is greater and what sin is uglier than to trade with religion in order to arrive through it at the achievement of personal aims and the satisfaction of personal lusts. . . .
>
> This situation which does away with stability and makes a person subject to another's whims arises from the degeneration of character which leads people to think lightly of faiths and religions. It further gives rise to iniquity which destroys the individual's faith in justice and makes people neither believe in the law nor honor its sanctity.

This whole question of conflict in jurisdiction caused the Court of Cassation, under the presidency of 'Abd al-'Azīz Fahmi, to digress, in a case involving the determination of what matters fell within "personal status," from the issues at hand to the entire problem of multiplicity of jurisdiction:[19]

> A person who follows the various stages of this case and sees that it has passed through the Coptic Millah Court, the Coptic Millah Court of Appeal, the National Court of First Instance, the National Court of Appeal, and the Court of Cassation, and that it will have to pass through the Sharī'ah Court in order to be referred again to the National Courts—such a person, if he is concerned with the interests of citizens, cannot but address the men in authority in this country that the time has long come for the unification of judicial jurisdiction so that the same judiciary would deal

[18] Anṭūn, pp. 19–20.

[19] Judgment 4 handed down June 21, 1934, and reported in *al-Muḥāmāh,* vol. 15, no. 3, December, 1934, pp. 87–96.

with questions of personal status for all Egyptians, Muslims and non-Muslims, as it now deals with questions of property, and that any hesitancy in the realization of this wish holds a great harm for the litigants and the interests of the country.

The third group of arguments against the personal-status courts might be called nationalistic ones. Here the concern was for "strengthening national unity by doing away with differences" between fellow citizens, "nurturing the feeling of social solidarity," and "realizing equality in word and deed among compatriots." The implication was that the various denominational courts were a powerful divisive factor in the country. Anṭūn apparently had this in mind when he said: "One of the fundamentals of Egyptian nationalism, and one of the means of removing differences between Egyptians, is the unification of the judiciary in the country, for the judiciary is the instrument of justice, and justice is the basis for moral and material advancement and one of the greatest factors in the establishment of national unity."[20] He also seems to have been, like many of his compatriots, especially sensitive to how the archaic types of jurisdictions might appear to foreign eyes at a time when Egypt wanted to look as modern as Europe:[21]

> Many a sigh do we give when we imagine a foreigner on his way from the Mixed Courts to the National Courts, then to the Sharī'ah Courts, then to the Consular Courts, then to the Ḥisbiyyah Courts, and then to the Millah Courts. In the latter he would meet the Egyptian and the Egyptianized; the be-hatted and the be-fezzed; those with black turbans and those with turbans of other colors; those who speak Arabic, Hebrew, Syraic, French, Latin, or Greek; those who apply Roman Law, Byzantine Law, or Torah Law, and those who are in a quandary as to what law to apply.

[20] Anṭūn, pp. 1, 5, 6.
[21] Anṭūn, p. 11.

The nationalist arguments tackled another aspect of this question: whether the existence of these courts was consistent with national sovereignty. It was vaguely understood and sometimes even asserted that the *millah* jurisdiction was akin to the capitulatory jurisdictions previously enjoyed by foreigners.[22] This understanding had a plausible basis in that the legal justification claimed for the *millah* jurisdictions was the supposed covenant given by the Caliph 'Umar to Sophronius, Bishop of Jerusalem, upon the conquest of that city in 638 A.D. by the Arabs, the religious and civil jurisdiction granted by Muḥammad II to the Patriarch of Constantinople upon the conquest of that city by the Ottomans, and the Hatti Humāyūn of 1856[23]—all instruments similar in conception and effect to international capitulatory treaties granting judicial privileges to foreigners. The protection given by some foreign powers to local minorities and their privileges served to confuse the two situations further. With the growth of ideas of territorial sovereignty and secular nationalism, a clearer line of demarcation had to be drawn between the two cases. Describing the special jurisdictions as they existed prior to their abolishment, Ḥāmid Zaki said:[24]

> It should not be forgotten that the capitulations which permit the *status quo* in relation to foreigners cannot justify it in relation to Egyptians who submit to the absolute

[22] Nasīm Sousa, *The Capitulatory Regime of Turkey: Its History, Origin, and Nature,* Baltimore, Md., 1933, pp. 89–112; Anṭūn, pp. 36–40.

[23] See Judgment 509 of the Cairo court of appeal handed down February 18, 1934, and reported in *al-Muḥāmāh,* vol. 15, no. 2, November, 1934, pp. 91–93, where this legal justification for *millah* jurisdictions was approved.

[24] Ḥāmid Zaki, pp. 797–798. Actually, the Egyptian government had exercised such a right in legislating for the Orthodox Copts (1883), the Native Anglicans (1902), and the Catholic Armenians (1905), and a precedent had been set. See Ṣalāḥ 'Abd al-Wahhāb, *Mudawwanat al-Aḥwāl al-Shakhṣiyyah li-ghayr al-Muslimīn,* Cairo, 1959, pp. 40–43.

authority of the law-giver. Yet it is certain that the law-giver has treated Egyptians in the same way, following a preexisting practice. There is no doubt, however, that this treatment was not based upon a preexisting obligation, for it cannot be said that the Egyptian non-Muslim communities have privileges which allow them to have special treatment. Custom in the Islamic countries had it that the Muslims and non-Muslims be equal in certain respects. In the same way that the former had recourse to their *sharīʻah* courts, the latter had recourse to their *millah* courts. What was intended, therefore, was equality in treatment in judicial matters, not the according of privileges to some Egyptians over others. Accordingly, if the Egyptian lawgiver should at any time be of the opinion that the continuance of this practice exposes public interest, or the interests of individuals belonging to these communities, to harm, he can change or amend the existing order of things.

Turning to the question of nationality and secular nationalism, Zaki emphasized that because these concepts then fashioned the bonds that drew the people together, and not religion, as had formerly been the case, "it is natural that any [legal] system based upon the ideas of religion should fade away, leaving the field open for the state and its sovereignty . . . and that everyone become subject to one judiciary, the state judiciary."[25]

[25] Zaki, p. 815. The opposition of conservative Muslim elements to abolishing the *sharīʻah* courts was no less severe than that of the non-Muslims to abolishing the *millah* courts. In 1930, when the "unification of the judiciary" was very much in the air, Rashīd Riḍā, the editor of *al-Manār,* wrote: "The enemies of Islamic law, and those resenting the Islamic hue of this country . . . renew their patent campaigns and their undercover intrigues to erase whatever is Islamic in it. Perhaps their aim . . . is preparing the way for demanding that Parliament abolish the Sharīʻah courts in the guise of 'unifying the judiciary.'" *Al-Manār,* vol. 30, no. 9, April, 1930, p. 779. In an interview in 1958 Shaykh ʻAbd al-Razzāq al-Qāḍi, the first and last president of the Sharīʻah Bar, said: "Unifying the courts was a mistake. The

Some lawyers even augmented their arguments against the personal-status courts with a program of reform. Aḥmad Ṣafwat, for instance, who had received his legal training in England, took his cue from the English Judicature Act of 1873, which unified the chancery and the common-law jurisdictions. He proposed that the *sharī'ah* courts form a division of the national courts, and that another division be created, composed initially of non-Muslim judges, to have concurrent jurisdiction with the *millah* courts, with the latter exercising their jurisdiction only with the consent of the parties to a dispute.[26] Farīd Anṭūn went even further, at least with regard to the *millah* courts. He proposed abolishing the *millah* courts altogether and transferring their jurisdiction to the national courts, which would then apply one code of personal status, preferably taken from the Swiss code, for all non-Muslims. He further urged the Committee on Personal Status, which had been created by the Ministry of Justice, to amend the rules of the *sharī'ah*, to do away with polygamy, and to limit the right of divorce so as to put an end to the two main enticements to changing religion.[27]

The Egyptian government was not unresponsive to these pleas, although it had to proceed with extreme caution to avoid offending the non-Muslim minorities. Attempts were made in 1931, 1936, 1942, and 1948 to reorganize the *millah* courts and to define their jurisdiction more clearly, but all these attempts failed in the end, mainly because of pressure by the *millah* authorities.[28] One such attempt, that made by the 'Ali Māhir cabinet in Decree 40 for the year 1936, seemed to go a long way

sharī'ah courts had a system different from that of the national courts. [Secular] law schools which staff the national courts are not adequate for teaching the *sharī'ah*. We [*sharī'ah* lawyers and judges] studied thirteen separate *sharī'ah* subjects, but in the law schools only superficial treatment is accorded to this study. As you can see, the *sharī'ah* requires specialization."

[26] Aḥmad Ṣafwat, *Iqtirāḥāt fi Iṣlāḥ Nuẓum al-Qaḍā'*, Cairo, 1929, pp. 42–43.

[27] Anṭūn, pp. 27, 33–36.

[28] *Cf.* George N. Sfeir, The Abolition of Confessional Jurisdiction in Egypt, *Middle East Journal,* vol. 10, no. 3, summer, 1956, p. 249.

toward ameliorating the situation by explicitly limiting the *millah* courts' jurisdiction to questions of marriage, divorce, and adoption, and by providing for a unified code of personal status for all non-Muslims, but this decree was annulled by the parliament during the tenure of the Naḥḥās cabinet which followed. The partial solution to this problem had to await the strong-arm revolutionary government of Jamāl 'Abd al-Nāṣir (Nasser), which, by Law 462 for the year 1955, completely abolished the *sharī'ah* courts and *millah* courts and transferred their jurisdiction to the national courts. The solution was not complete in that in dealing with questions of personal status the national courts continued to apply the *sharī'ah* for Muslims and the various laws of the denominations for non-Muslims,[29] thus continuing, albeit to a lesser extent, the possibilities of toying with conjugal rights and obligations through change of religion from one of the non-Muslim denominations to Islam.

It is interesting to note that the explanatory memorandum attached to the law repeated the arguments advanced earlier by the reformist lawyers for the unification of the courts: chaos in the *millah* courts, conflict of jurisdiction and delayed justice, the territorial sovereignty of the state, etc. There were two aspects of the law, however, which could not have pleased the reformist lawyers. The reformist lawyers had wanted one personal-status code, at least for all non-Muslims, but the various personal-status codes were retained. The memorandum justified this simply with the insistence that no violation should take place "with regard to the right of any group of Egyptians, whether Muslim or non-Muslim, in the application of its [special] law." The reformist lawyers had also insisted that a husband should not be allowed to change his obligations to his wife simply by changing his religion.[30] Apparently these two aspects of reform were left untouched for political, rather than strictly legal, rea-

[29] A presidential committee appointed to "review" the *sharī'ah* law of personal status could agree only on a draft not as liberal as those adopted in other Arab countries. This draft, however, has not been promulgated into law.

[30] See Ṣafwat, *Qaḍā'*, pp. 40–45; Anṭūn, p. 36.

sons, inasmuch as any change would have been widely unpopular. According to the new law, however, a change from one non-Muslim denomination to another during a court proceeding would not entail a change in the original law applicable to a dispute, but a change from a non-Muslim denomination to Islam would entail the application of Islamic law, which allows polygamy and easy divorce. The memorandum justified this discrepancy as follows:[31]

> [Article 7] is nothing but the application of a well-established doctrine, that the change in a person's religion entails that the person enjoy all the rights the new religion affords him. This doctrine itself is well established in the case of a change in nationality; the law-giver adopted it in Article 13, Paragraph 2, of the Civil Code, which provides that the law applicable to divorce is the law of the state to which the husband belongs at the time of the divorce. . . .

PERSONAL-STATUS LAW

Another aspect of legal reform that aroused national debate concerned those aspects of the *sharīʿah* that were being applied by the courts, the rules of personal status. There was no desire or practical reason, of course, for reforming the parts of the *sharīʿah,* such as the penal rules, that were not being applied and stood no chance of being applied. However, before any reform of particular *sharīʿah* rules could be considered, there was the primary issue of the possibility of changes in the *sharīʿah* at all. Here the reformers ran into a solid wall of resistence emanating from the nature of the *sharīʿah* itself. According to tradition, the *sharīʿah* was a body of rules which was to be valid "for every time and clime." No new interpretation (*ijtihād*) was to be attempted, as "the gate of *ijtihād*" was permanently blocked. It followed that "every innovation is a straying from the right path, and every such straying leads to Hell."

[31] Explanatory memorandum for Law 462 for the year 1955.

In such a rigid atmosphere reformers had to move very cautiously. There was no escaping the fact that the necessities of modern life required certain reforms, particularly in the laws of marriage, divorce, and inheritance but the reforms had to be carried out within an Islamic context and according to the rules of Islamic interpretation—even though the ideas behind them were Western—if they were to have any chance of adoption. Hence the great ingenuity of some reformers in reinterpreting the original *sharī'ah* sources—and even in disqualifying them as sources—and in reclassifying the various rules of the *sharī'ah* into religious and nonreligious, permanent and variable, in order to arrive at some sanction for the proposed reforms. And hence the changes in some rules of procedure in order to bring about practical changes in substantive rules, a course which proved even more effective.

The foremost modern Egyptian jurist, 'Abd al-Razzāq al-Sanhūri (Sanhoury), took up this problem in his *Le califat,* which was published in 1926, a time when demand for reform was very much in the air. He based his call for reform upon the need for complete equality between Muslims and non-Muslims —a thing which the *sharī'ah* did not concede—if non-Muslims were to be expected to accept the application of Muslim law to themselves, and upon the fact that the *sharī'ah* had not kept up with the requirements of modern civilization, particularly in the fields of economics and real property. The point of departure, he maintained, was a double process of separation, one between the religious and the temporal parts of the *sharī'ah* and the other between the permanent and the variable rules in the temporal parts. Presumably only the "variable rules" would be subject to change. Even in the temporal parts a further distinction was to be made between those parts having a religious coloring, which were to be binding only upon the conscience of Muslims, and those parts of a strictly juridical import which were to be binding on all persons.[32] Al-Sanhūri repeated this scheme for reform

[32] 'Abd al-Razzāq al-Sanhūri, *Le califat: son évolution vers une société des nations orientale,* Paris, 1926, pp. 578, 580–581.

at the International Congress for Comparative Law, held in August, 1932, at The Hague, and called upon the faculty of the Egyptian Law School to take the initiative in this reformist movement: "We must consider our problem just as important and just as vital for the Orient [Middle East] as was the movement of the rebirth of Roman law for Europe a few centuries ago."[33]

Whereas al-Sanhūri dealt generally with the problem of classification in order to facilitate reform, other lawyers attacked the hallowed bastions of the *sharī'ah* sources to this end. Not only were the well-known Traditions of the Prophet Muḥammad, on which legal precepts had been based, declared by some to be spurious, but even the Traditions that affirmed the infallibility of the Muslim community and enshrined the source of *ijmā'*, or consensus of the opinions on a matter, as the final arbiter in the interpretation of the Koran or the authenticity of a given Tradition were subject to attack. A more common attitude was to deny the existence of any true *ijmā'* in relevant instances, since, it was maintained, a true consensus had to be unanimous and expressed, two conditions which were virtually impossible after the Companions of the Prophet had scattered from Medina.[34]

Aḥmad Ṣafwat attempted to lay down a broad base for reform that for the most part disregarded the traditional sources of the *sharī'ah*. His views, as far as can be judged, represented those of a large segment of secular lawyers. Speaking at a meeting of the bar association in Alexandria on October 5, 1917, when the Ministry of Justice was considering some very cautious steps in the reform of personal-status law, Ṣafwat called for a bold program of action that would free the legislature from the shackles of casuistic interpretations of medieval scholars. As is customary in such situations, and to guard against a charge of infidelity, he prefaced his remarks with a reassertion of his

[33] 'Abd al-Razzāq al-Sanhūri, L'Université Égyptienne dans le Congrès International de Droit Comparé de la Haye, *Al-Qānūn wa-al-Iqtiṣād*, vol. 2, no. 5, November, 1932, pp. 289–312, esp. pp. 311–312.

[34] Anderson, Recent Developments, vol. 40, p. 255.

belief in Islam. However, the course he advocated was so progressive that it provoked severe attacks from conservative Muslims, and his relationship to Islam was questioned.[35]

Ṣafwat began with the assertion that modern generations were just as entitled to derive rules from the original sources of the *sharīʿah* as were the scholars and commentators of the third century A.H., when the principal schools of Islamic law were formed. He then took up the four main sources of the *sharīʿah*—the Koran, the *sunnah* or Traditions, *ijmāʿ* or consensus, and *qiyās* or analogy—and how far they could govern the derivation of rules. The *qiyās* he dismissed with the statement that modern generations could exercise analogy on the basis of rules derived from the other sources. *Ijmāʿ* could be either a consensus of scholars or a decision by someone previously in authority. He likened the consensus of scholars to the opinions of modern-law commentators, which can be effective only when adopted as law by the authorities concerned. The decisions of someone previously in authority, he maintained, could be abolished by his successor on the basis that the legislating authority could undo what it had previously done, with no attention to the identity of the authority at various times. The *sunnah* he divided into those Traditions that concerned individual instances, and were therefore limited to them, and those that were intended as general rules; in the latter case a Tradition was, in effect, "a law issued by the legislative authority; this same legislative authority would be possessed at any time afterwards by a ruler who could abolish what had been decreed previously." Ṣafwat was careful to limit this analysis to civil or nonreligious questions.[36]

Concerning the primary source of the *sharīʿah*, the Koran, Ṣafwat classified the rules derived from it into three categories:

[35] Aḥmad Ṣafwat, *Qāʿidat Iṣlāḥ Qānūn al-Aḥwāl al-Shakhṣiyyah*, Alexandria, 1917, p. 2; see Muḥammad Rashīd Riḍā, Madaniyyat al-Qawānīn, *al-Manār*, vol. 23, no. 7, July, 1922, pp. 539–548, esp. pp. 545–547.

[36] Ṣafwat, *Qāʿidat*, pp. 21, 22.

(1) rules which prohibit certain actions, (2) rules which make other actions obligatory, and (3) rules which declare a third variety of actions permissible.[37] Rules of the first category, such as those dealing with marriage within the prohibited degrees or to more than four wives, could not be altered or affected in any way. Rules of the second category, however, such as those concerning the completion of *'iddah,* the woman's period of retirement (three menstrual periods) before remarriage, or the presence of two witnesses at the conclusion of a marriage contract, could be maintained only to the extent and in the form that the reason for the rule would require. He reasoned that in these two examples, for instance, the rules were not obligatory for their own sake but rather for purposes to be realized by them—in the first case to insure that a woman was not pregnant at the time of remarriage and in the second to assure a certain measure of publicity for the marriage. If these purposes could be served by better and more direct means conforming to the requirements of the modern age—such as fixing a maximum of two years for *'iddah* (instead of waiting for the approximate time of menopause if the woman insisted, usually for the purposes of collecting alimony, that *'iddah* was not over) and providing for official registration of a marriage contract, a more effective means of publicity—then no end would be served in sticking to the letter of the Koranic provisions. The third category, that of permissible actions provided for in the Koran, could, like similar actions not so provided for, be practiced only in conformity with public interest. In the same way that a person could be prevented from practicing medicine or law without an official license, so could a person be prevented from marrying a second wife without a license. And just as a Muslim's right to own a slave had been prohibited, so could his right to divorce his wife be at least restricted. It followed, then, that only those provisions of the Koran which specifically prohibited certain actions were the ones that had

[37] Actually, this classification is a consolidation of the traditional categorization of actions in Islamic law into obligatory, recommended, free, disliked, and prohibited.

to be adhered to literally; the other provisions had to be understood and interpreted.[38]

Ṣafwat hoped that adoption of his thesis by the Ministry of Justice and the Personal Status Committee would clear the way for legislation introducing virtual monogamy, severe limits on divorce, and a greater voice for women in the selection of their husbands. However, the opposition of the conservative circles, and even of such Islamic modernists as Shaykh Muḥammad Rashīd Riḍā, made this practically impossible. Such an interpretation of the *sharīʿah* sources according to the tenets of Western legal theory was, in view of the differences in framework and methodology between the *sharīʿah* and Western legal systems, both naïve and infuriating to traditional elements.

The major points of Ṣafwat's proposed reforms were grouped under three propositions relating to personal-status law: (1) the freedom of the parties to a marriage contract and their equal obligation to it, (2) the removal of the contradiction between personal liberty as interpreted in the penal law and as interpreted in the law of personal status, and (3) making the contracts of marriage and divorce subject to official registration and control. With regard to the first proposition, Ṣafwat stressed that a wife could not have a stable position with the threat of divorce or of her husband marrying another wife constantly hanging over her head, and as a result she was forced to concentrate all her attention and energies on the strengthening of her position, to the neglect of the lofty purposes of marriage. Then, turning to the general law of contracts, he said that marriage was a bilateral contract to live together, and no party should be allowed to rescind this contract without the payment of damages which were usually payable upon the rescinding of far less important contracts, such as those relating to commerce and trade. Accordingly, he would strengthen the binding character of the marriage contract by severely limiting the right to

[38] Ṣafwat, *Qāʿidat,* pp. 20–30. See also on the same subject Aḥmad Ṣafwat, The Theory of Mohammedan Law, *Journal of Comparative Legislation and International Law,* vol. 2, 1920, pp. 310–316.

divorce, by making divorce exercisable only through the courts, and by extending it to both parties. He would also severely limit polygamy.[39] In relation to the discrepancy between penal law and personal-status law, Ṣafwat must have shocked his audience in pointing out the true legal situation, whereby a girl who had attained her majority was subject to having her marriage contract dissolved at the instance of her male agnates for a deficiency in her dower or for lack of social equality (*kafā'ah*) in the husband,[40] while they could not legally interfere, according to the Western-patterned penal code in the country, if she should without any semblance of marriage carry on intimate relations with any man. His point was that a girl should be free to choose her spouse without pressure or constraint by her family. The third proposition, making marriage and divorce subject to state registration, was to effect the desired stability and sanctity of the home, to guard against denial of the marital state, and to prevent third parties from mischievously interfering between the parties to a marriage contract.[41]

The questions of polygamy and divorce were also taken up by 'Abd al-Fattāḥ al-Sayyid, a law professor who later became president of the Court of Cassation. Writing in 1922, after some reforms had been carried out granting a woman judicial

[39] Ṣafwat, *Qā'idat*, pp. 6–7.

[40] See Farhat J. Ziadeh, Equality (*Kafā'ah*) in the Muslim Law of Marriage, *The American Journal of Comparative Law*, vol. 6, no. 4, October, 1957, pp. 503–517.

[41] Ṣafwat, *Qā'idat*, p. 8. To emphasize this last point Ṣafwat relates the following incident, which showed up the problems engendered by unregistered customary (*'urfi*) marriages: A notable from the Buḥayrah province held a big wedding party for his daughter. Just before the conclusion of the marriage contract the local *qāḍi* received a telegram from a spurned suitor of the daughter stating falsely that the girl had given herself unreservedly to him and that therefore she was his wife, and requesting that the *qāḍi* order the *ma'dhūn*, or local marriage official, not to go through with the new marriage contract. Under the circumstances the *qāḍi* had no alternative but to do what was requested of him until he had time to ascertain the facts, and the marriage party broke up amid heartaches. Naturally, such a situation could not have arisen had marriages been officially registered.

divorce under certain circumstances for nonmaintenance by the husband, for his long absence, or for his being afflicted with an "evil and incurable disease,"[42] al-Sayyid called further for a reinterpretation of certain verses in the Koran to limit polygamy to those cases where the wife was sick, old, or barren (with barrenness the determining factor), provided the husband could maintain two wives, and to make divorce exercisable at the hands of the court only after all efforts at reconciliation had failed.[43]

Pressure by these and other reformist lawyers brought about some noteworthy changes in the law of personal status. In addition to the law giving a woman the right to a judicial divorce, the Personal Status Committee formulated some other reforms which were adopted by the legislature. One, in effect, prescribed minimum ages for marriage, eighteen for males and sixteen for females.[44] Another gave a woman grounds for judicial divorce when she would "suffer harm" from the continuation of the marriage, or from the inexcusable absence of the husband for more than one year, or from his imprisonment for more than three years. It further restricted the formulas of divorce by the husband and provided that no claim could be entertained—whether for paternity, maintenance, or inheritance—if it were based on a period of gestation alleged to have lasted more than a solar year.[45] A third law provided that no claim concerning a marriage contracted after August 1, 1931, could be entertained unless the marriage were officially authenticated.[46] These reforms in the laws of marriage and divorce, although they were im-

[42] Law 25 dated July 12, 1920.

[43] See the review of al-Sayyid's book, *Ḥuqūq al-Mar'ah al-Mutazawwijah fi al-Islām* in *al-Muḥāmāh,* vol. 2, no. 10, July, 1922, pp. 521–523.

[44] Law 56, dated December 11, 1923.

[45] Law 25, dated March 10, 1929.

[46] Article 99 of Law 78, dated May 12, 1931. For details of these and other reforms see Anderson, Recent Developments; 'Abd al-Fattāḥ al-Sayyid, La Situation de la femme mariée Égyptienne après douze ans de réformes legislatives, *al-Qānūn wa-al-Iqtiṣād,* vol. 2, no. 2, March, 1932, pp. 65–82.

portant, were all that was possible under the method of reform adopted by the Personal Status Committee, which included several *ulema* of al-Azhar. The committee's necessarily eclectic approach was based on practical solutions to individual problems instead of an honest and forthright reinterpretation of the *sharīʿah*—according to Islamic principles, to be sure—in conformity with modern exigencies. Some elements of this approach were reminiscent of the *ḥiyal,* devices employed by medieval Muslim jurists to circumvent a strict law in favor of a liberal course more in conformity with the requirements of daily living.

The whole reform movement was based upon the assertion that the ruler (or, in a modern state, the legislature) could, according to Islamic law, restrict the jurisdiction of the courts not only with regard to locale and time, but also with regard to what cases might be heard and which of the variant views of jurists could be applied.[47] Child marriages, for instance, were virtually eliminated by forbidding the courts to entertain any claim with regard to any marriage in which the parties had not been of minimum age at the time of marriage. Since only a foolhardy father or marriage guardian would consent to the marriage of his ward without the future protection of the law, the result was reform of the law through a procedural measure.[48] Similarly, when the courts were forbidden to entertain any claim —whether for paternity, maintenance, or inheritance—based on a period of gestation alleged to have lasted more than a solar year, the reform was effected through a procedural means. The restriction of the courts to the views of certain jurists on specific issues as embodied in special legislation (regardless of whether

[47] Anderson, Recent Developments, vol. 40, p. 254.

[48] Although this measure was supported by several *ulema,* including the current Mufti of Egypt and the rector of al-Azhar, it was severely attacked by Shaykh Muḥammad Bakhit, the ex-Mufti, on the ground that the jurisdiction of a *qāḍi* (court) could be only restricted for a stated public interest and with the further proviso that some other *qāḍi* would exercise the excluded jurisdiction; see his article Taḥdīd Sinn al-Zawāj, *al-Muḥāmāh,* vol. 4, no. 4, January, 1924, pp. 399–411, esp. p. 409.

those views represented a minority opinion among the jurists of the official rite, the Ḥanafi, or whether they belonged to jurists of other *sunni* rites, or even to extinct rites, or whether they were a combination of several views) made it possible for some ill-used wives to obtain judicial divorce and placed some restrictions on the validity of formulas of divorce pronounced by Muslim husbands.[49] In the field of inheritance and testamentary dispositions the opinions of some early jurists were incorporated in a reform which provided for "obligatory bequests" to grandchildren from their grandparents, if the parents had predeceased them, to the extent of what the parents would have inherited on intestacy had they survived, provided the bequests did not exceed one-third of the estates. Previously such grandchildren had been totally excluded by their uncles. Even a Shīʿah view was adopted, although not openly, whereby a Muslim was empowered to make bequests within the bequeathable third to any of his heirs, an action which had not been possible under *sunni* law except with the consent of the other heirs.[50]

At this point the devices employed to effect reform had apparently been exhausted, as predicted by Ṣafwat in 1917, when he proposed his theory of reform and criticized the method then pursued by the Ministry of Justice of justifying individual reforms by the opinion of some medieval jurist. This device, he claimed, made the task of the reform committee interminable and rendered it impossible for the committee "to arrive at solutions for some evils because these solutions are of recent origin and could not have occurred to any of the jurists a thousand years ago."[51] There are still a myriad of problems that await solution. For instance, there is nothing in the law that prevents a man from divorcing his wife at will or from taking up

[49] See Anderson, *Islamic Law,* p. 29.

[50] Law 71, dated July 1, 1946, Articles 37 and 76–79. For a detailed justification of the "obligatory bequest" see H. M. ʿAzzām, al-Waṣiyyah al-Wājibah, *al-Muḥāmāh,* vol. 37, no. 8, April, 1957, pp. 1046–1060.

[51] Ṣafwat, *Qāʿidat,* p. 19.

to four wives.[52] Because of the emphasis on agnates, the estate of a man leaving a daughter and a distant agnate is still divided equally between the two heirs, although the man may not even have known his distant agnate or may have disliked him thoroughly. Some modern reformers would equalize the inheritance shares of Muslim males and females,[53] although the Koran specifically makes a male's share double that of a female.[54] Solutions to these problems and many similar ones may require a reinterpretation by modern Muslim scholars of the fundamental texts in accordance with modern needs, with the frank espousal

[52] Attempts to limit polygamy and a husband's right to divorce his wife at will have so far failed. The draft of Law 25 for the year 1920 included two articles that would make marriage to a second wife dependent upon the consent of the *qāḍi,* and would require the *qāḍi* not to give that consent except to a man who was capable of happy conjugal relations and of maintaining those who were already dependent upon him. Those two articles, although approved by the *ulema* members of the Personal Status Committee, were deleted because of strong opposition from other *ulema.* Almost identical provisions were included in a draft of a law prepared in 1945 by the Ministry of Social Affairs. This draft also included provisions that would require a man to obtain the permission of the *qāḍi* to divorce his wife, and would require the *qāḍi* not to grant permission unless he had ascertained the causes of discord and had failed in his attempts to reconcile the couple. Noncompliance with these last provisions would make the man liable to a fine or imprisonment, although his unilateral action in divorcing his wife would be effective. This draft law also failed to reach the statute books because of opposition. Shaykh Muḥammad Abu Zahrah, in Mashrū' al-Qānūn al-Khāṣṣ bi-Taqyīd al-Ṭalāq wa-Ta'addud al-Zawjāt, *al-Qānūn wa-al-Iqtiṣād,* vol. 15, nos. 1–3, January–March, 1945, pp. 125–184, disapproved of both provisions; Shaykh 'Abd al-Wahhāb Khallāf, al-Sharī'ah al-Islāmiyyah wa-al-Shu'ūn al-Ijtimā'iyyah, *al-Qānūn wa-al-Iqtiṣād,* vol. 17, no. 1, March, 1947, pp. 137–158, approved of the provisions against polygamy and disapproved of those limiting divorce.

[53] See the suggestion made by the Egyptian publicist-statesman, Maḥmūd 'Azmi and the attack on him by Muḥammad Rashīd Riḍā in *al-Manār,* vol. 30, no. 9, April, 1930, pp. 698–709.

[54] Koran, 4:11.

of the principle that changes in circumstances should bring about changes in the law.

WAQF LAW

Closely related to questions of personal status—and considered by some modern jurists as part of the personal-status issues—is the matter of *waqfs,* or perpetual endowments,[55] either for charitable purposes or for the benefit of one's family. The reform of the law related to these endowments evoked perhaps more controversy and heated debate than any other aspect of legal reform. The reasons are not too hard to find. In the first place, since the beneficiaries of charitable *waqfs* were mosques, religious schools, and the like, and since such institutions were almost always the ultimate beneficiaries of even family *waqfs,* *waqfs* were always popularly associated with religion, and any criticism of this institution was construed by conservative elements as directed against religion. In the second place, there were many people, especially the managers of *waqf* properties and *sharī'ah* lawyers, whose material interests were tied to this institution (the former received regular salaries, while the latter depended chiefly on *waqf* cases for their livelihood) and who fought tooth and nail against the proposals to modify it. On the other side of the issue, the secular lawyers who were demanding abolishment of the family *waqf* were emboldened by the fact that the institution could claim no direct sanction in the Koran and that various medieval jurists had held conflicting opinions regarding its fundamental precepts.

The demands of Egyptian lawyers during the period from 1910 to 1930 for abolishing, or at least modifying, the family *waqf* were preceded, and possibly influenced, by actions against family endowments in Europe and even in Egypt itself. The

[55] For a statement of the law of *waqf* and its comparison to the law of trusts in Anglo-American law see M. Khadduri and H. J. Liebesny (eds.), *Law in the Middle East,* Washington, 1955, pp. 203–222.

leveling influence of the French Revolution and the revolutionary movements of the nineteenth century had an adverse effect on the strongholds of privilege, including family endowments. Liberals started to view these endowments as one way of perpetuating the position of priveleged classes, and, quite understandably, subjected the institution to censure. A similar attitude toward *waqfs* was adopted by young Ottoman reformers who had been deeply influenced by European ideas and called for the abolishment of an institution which, they claimed, hindered financial dealings and retarded economic progress.[56] In Egypt Muḥammad 'Ali, influenced by Ottoman ideas of reform and surrounded by a host of European reformers, tackled the matter of *waqfs* with a view to their complete annulment; such an end not only would effect economic reform, but would supplement his treasury with taxes which were currently going to the various purposes of the *waqfs*. Accordingly, he began with what was known as "untrue *waqf*," or *waqf* of *kharāji* (state-owned) land. This he abolished completely in 1813, when he did away with the institution of *iltizām* (collection of taxes through *multazims*, or tax farmers), which had embraced all *kharāji* lands, and ordered the peasants to pay their taxes directly to the government. Three decades later he started eyeing the "true *waqfs*," which embraced buildings and agricultural lands within the complete ownership (*milk*) of the founders. In this area, however, he had to move with caution because of the sanctity this type of *waqf* had acquired throughout the ages. He therefore elicited a *fatwa* (legal opinion) from Shaykh Muḥammad ibn Maḥmūd al-Jazāyirli, Mufti of Alexandria, to the effect that the person in authority could prevent owners from constituting their properties into *waqfs* to safeguard against the corrupt practice of using the institution to exclude heirs and to defeat the claims of creditors who might wish to follow the properties in order to satisfy their debts. He then issued a decree in 1845 forbidding

[56] Muḥammad Aḥmad Faraj al-Sanhūri, *Majmū'at al Qawānīn al-Miṣriyyah al-Mukhtārah min al-Fiqh al-Islāmi,* vol. III, Cairo, 1949, p. 7.

forthwith the constitution of new *waqfs*. The old *waqfs* continued, however, and new ways were found to constitute others. Finally a succession of decrees in later years allowed the constitution of *waqfs* in all types of land.[57]

In the early 1900s, when the campaign against family endowments was renewed in Europe,[58] a similar campaign was unleashed in Egypt against *waqfs*. In 1898 Qāsim Amīn, in his book *Asbāb wa-Natā'ij wa-Akhlāq wa-Mawā'iẓ* (*Causes and Effects: Ethics and Sermons*), had criticized family *waqfs* and the motives of their founders. His disapproval of *waqfs* in general was reflected in the adamant stand he had once taken against the creation of a particular *waqf*. While serving as a member of the board of the Islamic Benevolent Society, he had opposed the suggestion of another member to constitute all the properties of the society into a *waqf*. When he found that the majority favored the proposal, he chose to resign his position rather than submit to a decision that ran counter to one of his basic beliefs. In the face of such a strong stand the majority retracted their decision and did not return to their previous position even after Amīn's death in 1908.[59] A similar stand was taken by 'Azīz Khānki. Although he was a Christian, he engaged during the autumn of 1903 in a prolonged debate on the pages of *al-Muqaṭṭam* with Shaykh Muḥammad Rashīd Riḍā', the editor of *al-Manār*, over the question of whether the *waqf* was a part of the Islamic religion; Khānki maintained that *waqf* could

[57] Al-Sanhūri, *Majmū'at*, pp. 8–10; Muḥammad 'Ali 'Allūbah, *Mabādi' fi al-Siyāsah al-Miṣriyyah*, Cairo, 1942, pp. 294–297; the *fatwa* of al-Jazāyirli is reproduced on p. 295.

[58] The laws of several European countries either outlawed or greatly limited family endowments. Article 335 of the Swiss Civil Code of 1912 forbade the setting up of these endowments, while Article 155 of the German Constitution of 1919 abolished them. In England the rule of the common law against perpetuities was modified and clarified by the Law of Property Act of 1925. In Turkey *waqfs* were abolished in 1926, even before the adoption of the Swiss civil code.

[59] Ibrāhīm al-Hilbāwi, Rijāl al-Qaḍā' al-Rāḥilūn, in *al-Kitāb al-Dhahabi lil-Maḥākim al-Ahliyyah*, vol. I, Cairo, 1937, p. 485.

claim no authority in the Koran or the Traditions, and Riḍā' asserted that the Traditions gave the institution strong support.[60] Since Khānki's opinions were expressed in connection with a specific *waqf* case decided by a *sharī'ah* court, he was disciplined by the appropriate disciplinary board, which suspended him from pleading before that court for six months.[61] His criticism of family *waqfs* continued, and after the subject was broached by a parliamentary committee in 1926, he called for their complete abolishment, basing his demands on the Islamic-law maxim that necessity renders prohibited things permissible.[62]

Muṣṭafa Ṣabri, an admirer and legal colleague of Khānki, also opposed family *waqfs,* and when he ventured to express his opinions in 1918, he was dubbed by conservative elements a *zindīq* (heretic) and *kāfir* (infidel).[63] Five years later he published a booklet in which he stated that family *waqfs* violated the inheritance verses in *sūrah* 4 of the Koran, that such early jurists as Shurayḥ and Ismā'īl al-Kindi had considered *waqfs* illegal, and that they should therefore be abolished. To augment his argument Ṣabri presented the earlier *fatwa* of Shaykh al-Jazāyirli and decree of Muḥammad 'Ali as precedents.[64]

All these writings and the similar ones they evoked in the daily press, plus the fact that a law had just been passed in Turkey prohibiting *waqfs,* prompted the Waqf Committee of the House of Deputies to say in its report on the budget of the Ministry of Waqfs for the year 1927 that "It is incumbent upon Parliament and those at the helm of economic and social affairs in the country to consider whether it is advisable to

[60] See an account of this debate in *al-Manār,* vol. 6, no. 17, November, 1903, pp. 816–819, no. 18, December, 1903, pp. 729–736.

[61] Muṣṭafa Ṣabri, Ḍarūrat Ilghā' al-Awqāf al-Ahliyyah, *al-Muḥāmāh,* vol. 7, no. 6, March, 1927, p. 751.

[62] Article by Khānki in *al-Muqaṭṭam,* February 12, 1928, as reproduced in 'Azīz Khānki, *Aḥādith,* Cairo, n.d., pp. 22–24.

[63] Ṣabri, Ḍarūrat, p. 752.

[64] Muṣṭafa Ṣabri, *Iqtirāḥāt fi Ilghā' al-Awqāf al-Ahliyyah,* Cairo, 1923.

continue the family-*waqf* system or not." However, when the fiery lawyer and deputy 'Abd al-Ḥamīd 'Abd al-Ḥaqq demanded the total abolishment of family *waqfs,* the ensuing hot debate between his supporters and the defenders of the *waqf* system resulted in the rejection of a proposal to form a committee to study the question.[65]

The cause of the opponents of family *waqfs* was further strengthened when Muḥammad 'Ali 'Allūbah, an able lawyer and former Minister of Waqfs, assumed leadership of their movement. Through lectures, articles in the daily press, and parliamentary debates over proposed measures to abolish family *waqfs* or limit them to a stated period of years, this group strove to persuade public opinion that *waqfs* had nothing to do with religion and that the evils of the system far outweighed any benefits it might have. Two lectures delivered by 'Allūbah, one in Arabic to the National Bar Association at the headquarters of the Cairo court of appeal in 1926 and the other in French at the headquarters of the mixed courts in Cairo in 1927, summed up the arguments of this group.[66]

'Allūbah followed Muṣṭafa Ṣabri's earlier contention that there was no connection between family *waqfs* and religion. The only kind of *waqf* envisioned by the Traditions, he asserted, was the charitable variety which would benefit the poor or serve "in the path of God." This was the reason, he asserted, that jurists insisted that family *waqfs,* to be legal, must contain provisions for an ultimate benefit to charity in case the first purposes should fail, even though the founders might not have

[65] Session of the House of Deputies on September 8, 1926, p. 866, as quoted in al-Sanhūri, *Majmū'at,* pp. 12–13.

[66] Muḥammad 'Ali 'Allūbah, Fi al-Waqf, *al-Muḥāmāh,* vol. 7, no. 4, January, 1927, pp. 309–320; Le problème du wakf, *L'Égypte contemporaine,* vol. 18, nos. 102–103, November–December, 1927, pp. 501–524. A French translation of the first lecture is given in *L'Égypte contemporaine,* vol. 18, no. 101, May, 1927, pp. 385–402, and an answer by Shaykh Muḥammad Bakhit, a former Mufti of Egypt, entitled De l'institution du wakf (translated from the Arabic) is on pp. 403–431.

seriously considered such a possibility. It followed that family *waqfs* were a purely civil matter, like a sale or any other transaction, and could be regulated in order to correct their abuses.

'Allūbah described the abuses and drawbacks of the *waqf* institution as follows. First, the continued creation of *waqfs* could result in tying up real estate and proportionately decreasing the property that could be pledged as security for financial transactions, thus decreasing the wealth of the country. He estimated that 11 percent of the lands under agriculture were *waqf* lands and that this percentage was fast increasing.[67] Family *waqfs,* by their very nature, continued from generation to generation. Since in most cases the members of succeeding generations numbered more than those of earlier ones, the number of beneficiaries increased continually, thereby decreasing the yearly share of each to a ridiculously small amount,[68] while the share of the manager, who in many cases was not even a descendent of the founder, continued to be the same. Another problem was that beneficiaries forsook all work, depending solely upon their meager share in the *waqf* income. As a result they became indigent and fell prey to usurers to whom they assigned their future shares.[69] Moreover, the tying up of property in a family *waqf* hindered the energetic descendents of the founder from using the *waqf* property in enterprises that could have benefited them and the country alike. It was common knowledge in Cairo that *waqf* buildings were generally neglected and in a state of dilapidation and hence netted far less income than "free" buildings.[70]

[67] 'Allūbah, Fi al-Waqf, p. 314. Khānki's estimate was 10 percent. See his Niẓām al-Waqf, *al-Muḥāmāh,* vol. 7, nos. 9–10, June–July, 1927, p. 942. In 1940 *waqf* lands amounted to 662,700 *feddans;* see 'Allūbah, *Mabādi',* p. 301.

[68] In 1927 the beneficiaries of a certain *waqf* in Alexandria numbered 438 persons, with each receiving 60 piasters, although the income was £E7,500 yearly; 'Allūbah, *Mabādi',* p. 301.

[69] Law 60 for the year 1942 restricted such assignment within narrow limits.

[70] 'Allūbah, Fi al-Waqf, pp. 313–318.

'Allūbah characterized the intention of the founder to preserve the corpus of his property for his descendents as a fleeting hope in view of the actual state of affairs, but he gave weight to the motive of remedying certain deficiencies in the laws of inheritance and testamentary dispositions through the use of *waqfs*. Many founders wanted to provide for a descendent excluded by the laws of inheritance (such as a daughter's son in competition with a distant agnate, or a grandson in competition with his paternal uncle) or to favor one heir over another, since there were provisions against making a bequest to an heir.[71] Accordingly, 'Allūbah proposed that the institution be retained as long as the laws of inheritance and testamentary dispositions continued in force, but only in a modified form that would obviate its abuses. Specifically, he proposed limiting family *waqfs* to a certain period of years or to the end of a specified generation, with the property going at the end of this period to the beneficiaries in the proportion of their shares in the yearly income. He also proposed dissolving family *waqfs* that had already exceeded the specified period.[72] He actually presented a bill to this effect to the parliament early in 1927, but it was not adopted, nor was another bill presented by two of his colleagues to abolish *waqfs* completely.[73] The opposition raised by Muslim religious circles, in the form of public lectures by Shaykh Bakhīt and a public statement signed by 460 teachers in al-Azhar and other religious schools, was instrumental in temporarily halting the movement for reform.

In 1936 the Waqf Committee of the Chamber of Deputies returned to the attack and proposed legislation that would prohibit the constitution of any new family *waqf* and would limit the properties of charitable *waqfs*. This proposal was sidetracked, however, by the formation, on December 9, 1936, of a Personal Status Committee, composed of *ulema* and secular

[71] This was changed later by Article 37 of Law 71 for the year 1946.

[72] 'Allūbah, Fi al-Waqf, p. 318–320.

[73] Al-Sanhūri, *Majmū'at,* p. 13.

lawyers, to prepare a comprehensive code of personal status and such related matters as *waqfs,* inheritance, and testamentary dispositions. The results of the committee's labors were the Law of Inheritance (Law 77 for the year 1943), the Law of Testamentary Dispositions (Law 71 for the year 1946), and the Law of the Rules of Waqf (Law 48 for the year 1946). This last law incorporated some of the ideas previously advanced by 'Allūbah and his colleagues and provided, almost without precedent, that any future *waqf* (except a mosque or cemetery) would continue to be revocable by its founder, that any charitable *waqf* (except one in support of a mosque) might in the future be either permanent or temporary, and that family *waqfs* should henceforth last no more than sixty years or two generations after the death of the founder. Certain other reforms touching upon a variety of points which had given rise to complaint were carried out, although in most cases the reformers had to seek refuge in the opinion of some medieval jurist, or even a combination of opinions, that could be construed as agreeing with modern requirements.[74]

Although the secular lawyers were not completely successful in their campaign to abolish family *waqfs,* they got most of the reforms they had been clamoring for, and the conservative elements could point out with pride that one of the main institutions of the *sharī'ah* had been kept intact in form if not in content. With minor exceptions, there was general contentment with the compromise solution. Even the Lebanese followed the Egyptian example in the reform of their family *waqfs* in 1947. Nevertheless, the revolutionary government which came to power in Egypt in July, 1952, completely abolished family *waqfs* that autumn by Law 180. In the explanatory memorandum accompanying the law, dated September 14, 1952, the abolishment of family *waqfs* was tied to the earlier Agrarian Reform Law, which had limited individual land holding to 200 *feddans* and provided for the distribution of land to peasants. Since many family *waqfs* consisted of extensive agricultural acreage, *waqfs* had to be

[74] For details see Anderson, Recent Developments, vol. 42, 1952.

abolished to make the agrarian reform more effective and to permit all types of land to be treated on an equivalent basis. The memorandum also advanced the economic arguments which had been leveled against family *waqfs* by two generations of lawyers. No attempt was made to justify the reform in terms of the *sharīʿah* or the opinion of any individual authority. The temperament of the new military regime was alien to the casuistic approach; all the memorandum said in this regard was that the freeing of the property opened up the field of dignified labor to the poor, which is "the highest form of righteousness and approach to God."

THE CIVIL CODE

The reform of the civil code evoked, surprisingly enough, almost as much discussion and heated debate as the reform of the *waqf* system. It might seem that this code, patterned after the French civil code and set forth in 1883, would have been so deeply entrenched in both theory and practice that when the time came for its reform there would be little likelihood of a move for its replacement by any completely new code, let alone one based on Islamic law. The civil law, unlike the law of personal status, was not even remotely connected with religion, so that no religious motives were involved; moreover, as early as 1926 Turkey had found its civil code based on Islamic law (the Majallah) to be unworkable and had replaced it by the Swiss code. Hence it is surprising that there would be a proposal at this date to base the economic life of the country upon medieval legal precepts innocent of any adjustment to modern needs. However, several circumstances combined to make this proposal into a serious challenge to those secular lawyers who wanted a code based partly on Islamic law, but with its major provisions derived from the previous code and other European models.

The very existence in Cairo of al-Azhar University, the

guardian of Muslim learning, seemed to impose on Egypt the moral duty of championing Islamic matters. Some considered it futile for al-Azhar and the Egyptian University to continue to teach the *sharīʿah* while it was being largely ignored in formulating the country's codes. Moreover, the detailed formulation of *sharīʿah* rules by medieval jurists was, in nationalist views, a manifestation of the "Arab genius" which should be used in the rejuvenation of the entire Arab world and the unification of its laws. The current aura of national pride caused even the secular lawyers to sing the glory of the *sharīʿah.* Following the early researches of Western orientalists in the *sharīʿah,* many law students educated in French universities had written their theses on some aspect of Islamic law and invariably pointed out its excellence in comparison even with modern systems. The interest of these scholars persuaded the International Congress of Comparative Law in 1938 to declare the *sharīʿah* as one of the independent sources for the study of comparative law. The Egyptian delegation at the Washington conference, held in April, 1945, to consider the constitution of the Permanent Court of International Justice, availed themselves of this opportunity to press for the appointment of a judge who represented the *sharīʿah* (Islamic countries) at this court, a demand which resulted in the appointment of ʿAbd al-Ḥamīd Badawi to that august office.[75] Under these circumstances it seemed somewhat incongruous that the *sharīʿah,* which was being respected abroad, should be ignored at home. An additional factor was that during the 1930s and 1940s, when the reform of the civil code was being actively pursued, the society known as the Muslim Brotherhood had gained strength among all segments of the population, including lawyers and judges. One of its fundamental tenets was that all laws should be derived from, or at least be consonant with, the Koran, and that it was useless to debate the reform of the civil code as long as this principle had not been

[75] See Naqd li-Mashrūʿ al-Qānūn al-Madani, by a committee of *ulema* and lawyers in *al-Muḥāmāh,* special issue, March, 1948, pp. 22–23.

agreed upon.[76] In other words, the brotherhood wanted a code based on the *sharī'ah.*

The controversy started in 1936, when, in anticipation of the eventual disappearance of the mixed courts, a committee was formed to revise the code with a view toward making it the sole code for all civil issues except personal status. Another committee was then appointed to codify the law of personal status, and it was the famous jurist 'Abd al-Razzāq al-Sanhūri who took the initiative in formulating the principles of reform and actually codifying a new civil law and seeing it through legislation. Just before the committee was appointed, on the occasion of the fiftieth anniversary of the national courts, al-Sanhūri wrote a book-length article emphasizing the need for reform and suggesting the lines along which it should proceed.[77]

There was little quarrel in Egyptian legal circles over the need for extensive reform of the old code. As much as it had accomplished in correcting a chaotic situation in the field of civil law, its defects had become all too apparent with time. Its blind imitation of the French code resulted in duplication of some of the latter's defects without the jurisprudential reforms introduced by the French judiciary. What is more, in areas where the *sharī'ah* law of personal status overlapped civil laws, there was no explicit provision as to which law applied. For instance, it was problematical for some time which law was

[76] See the remarks of Ḥasan al-Huḍaybi, who later became the leader of the society, in Naqd li-Mashrū', insert leaf before p. 3, and 'Abd al-Qādir 'Awdah, *al-Islām wa-Awḍā'una al Qānūniyyah,* Cairo, 1951. For an account of the history and tenets of this religio-political society see Isḥāq Mūsa al-Ḥusayni, *The Moslem Brethren* (tr. by John F. Brown and John Racy), Beirut, 1956; and Christina Phelps Harris, *Nationalism and Revolution in Egypt: The Role of the Muslim Brotherhood,* The Hague, 1967.

[77] 'Abd al-Razzāq al-Sanhūri, Wujūb Tanqīḥ al-Qānūn al-Madani, *al-Qānūn wa-al-Iqtiṣād,* vol. 6, no. 1, January, 1936, pp. 3–144. A shorter version of this article appears under the title 'Ala Ayy Asās Yakūn Tanqīḥ al-Qānūn al-Madani al-Miṣri, in *al-Kitāb al-Dhahabi lil-Maḥākim al-Ahliyyah,* vol. II, Cairo, 1938, pp. 106–143.

applicable to the devolution of inherited property—the *sharī'ah* principle which held that there could be no inheritance before the payment of the deceased's debts, or the French principle which held that the deceased's rights and obligations passed to his heirs.[78] Similarly, it was not clear for some time what the period of prescription relative to *waqf* lands was—thirty-three years as provided by the *sharī'ah*, which simply barred claims against the possessor, or fifteen years as provided by civil law, which granted him outright ownership. These defects were not of great moment, however, in comparison with the fact that the strides made by the science of comparative jurisprudence since 1883 had left the civil code far behind. This was especially true with regard to general theories relating to such matters as the abuse of rights, fraud, legal persons, vicarious responsibility, defense of nonperformance by the other party, transfer of debts, and obligations assumed unilaterally. Additional defects were vague texts, contradictions, faulty translations from the French, and inexact wording.[79]

Al-Sanhūri proposed the appointment of a committee to codify the entire field of civil law, including personal status. Personal-status law was to be based on the *sharī'ah* but to be so designed as to be suitable for non-Muslims as well. The other provisions of the code, those dealing with obligations, were to be derived from the jurisprudence of the Egyptian courts,

[78] For the controversy on this point which affected the rights of a bona fide purchaser for value from an heir, see 'Ali Zaki al-'Urabi, Markaz al-Wārith fi al-Qawānīn al-Miṣriyyah, *al-Muḥāmāh,* vol. 1, no. 5, November, 1920, pp. 225–237, which was an answer to a lecture by A. 'Abd al-Laṭīf with the same title, printed later in *al-Muḥāmāh,* vol. 2, no. 3, December, 1921, pp. 113–131. The latter's support of the French law principle as against that of the *sharī'ah* gained him some unkind words. 'Abd al-Ḥamīd Badawi, La Tarikah illa ba'd Dayn, *al-Muḥāmāh,* vol. I, nos. 8, 9, February–March, 1921, pp. 369–376, 433–439, supported the *sharī'ah* principle.

[79] For a discussion of all these defects see 'Abd al-Razzāq al-Sanhūri, Wujūb Tanqīḥ al-Qānūn al-Madani, *al-Qānūn wa-al-Iqtiṣād,* vol. 6, January, 1936, pp. 24–42.

from the modern codes of other countries, and from the *sharī'ah.* By "jurisprudence of the Egyptian courts" al-Sanhūri meant those aspects of the law which had been neglected by the old code and which the courts had developed in their decisions, such as collective ownership, easements, third-party interests in contracts, and stipulations for penal damages. From the *sharī'ah,* which he characterized as "one of the superior systems of law in the world," he proposed taking not only those provisions which had been adopted by the old code and the principles accepted by the courts as forming a part of the law, but also many new provisions relating both to general principles and to specifics.[80] This interest in the *sharī'ah* was not merely a reflection of the demands of conservative elements for basing the new code exclusively on the *sharī'ah;*[81] al-Sanhūri's own works demonstrate that it was, rather, a genuine effort to incorporate in the body of law as much as was feasible of a great heritage.[82]

The utilization of the *sharī'ah* as only a supplement to other sources was unacceptable to the traditional groups, particularly those trained in *sharī'ah* law. It was barely two months after the publication of al-Sanhūri's article and one month after the appointment of the committee to revise the code that Shaykh Muḥammad Sulaymān, a judge in the supreme *sharī'ah* court, called, in a public lecture delivered on March 31, 1936, for making the *sharī'ah* the sole basis of the new civil code. This lecture must have had considerable impact in view of the wide circulation and comments in the press.[83] Sulaymān, after a long introduction which endeavored to show that the *sharī'ah* was suitable for application in modern times, lamented the fact that in the Ottoman Empire in the period of the Tanẓīmāt the Turks

[80] Al-Sanhūri, Wujūb, pp. 111–142.

[81] Naqd li-Mashrū', pp. 24–25.

[82] Al-Sanhūri, *Le califat.* His later works include *Maṣādir al Ḥaqq fi al-Fiqh al-Islāmi,* Cairo, 1954–1958, an extensive study of rights in the *sharī'ah.*

[83] Bi-Ayy Shar' Nukḥam?, *Égypte contemporaine,* vol. 27, no. 163, April, 1936, pp. 289–365, esp. the comments quoted on pp. 363–365.

had adopted European laws and that in Egypt in 1883 the *sharī'ah,* which had held sway for thirteen centuries, had been displaced by European codes.[84] With the appointment of a committee in March, 1936, to revise the civil code he saw an opportunity to correct this lapse by returning to the *sharī'ah.* He cited both the Ottoman Majallah and the works of Qadri Pasha as proof that the *sharī'ah* could be codified to avoid the necessity of consulting the works of medieval jurists with their intricate language and inadequate arrangement of material.[85]

It is indicative of the emotional appeal of the *sharī'ah* as a "national" product that Sulaymān's first reason for advocating its restoration was not his religious belief, but what he called the "dictate of patriotism." He considered a nation to be distinguished from all other nations by its individual characteristics, chief among which is its jurisprudence. In answer to the assertion of the president of the committee that the legislation then obtaining in Egypt was in accord with the spirit of the nation, Sulaymān declared: "Upon my life, that legislation is not of the nation's womb; it is merely an adopted one. Its real son who is set aside has not been forgotten, for *he* is its natural spirit." The second reason Sulaymān gave was religion, language, and tradition, deference to which would require the reestablishment of the *sharī'ah* in Egypt. Other significant arguments were the hope that the *sharī'ah* would be a unifying force among the Middle Eastern states if they also adopted it as their basic legislation, the fact that the best legislation is one which people observe out of inner conviction, and the fact that the *sharī'ah* was a jurisprudential treasure which would go to waste if it were not utilized.[86]

[84] Bi-Ayy Shar' Nukḥam?, pp. 328–329. *Tanẓīmāt* is the name given to the various legal and administrative reforms which were introduced in the Ottoman Empire starting with the Imperial Rescript of 1839.

[85] Bi-Ayy Shar' Nukḥam?, pp. 331, 335. For Qadri's achievements see Chapter 1.

[86] Bi-Ayy Shar' Nukḥam?, p. 345–353.

The divergent views of those who wanted the *sharī'ah* merely to supplement other sources in the formulation of the new code and those who wanted it to be the exclusive, or at least the dominant, source must have been very much in the minds of the committee appointed to restudy the civil code. It appears, however, that in view of the consistently secular and progressive history of legislation in Egypt since the period of Muḥammad 'Ali, neither this committee nor the two that supplanted it seriously considered complete restoration of *sharī'ah* law as a new code. Even when al-Sanhūri, one of the two members of the third committee, presented the draft of the new code to an assemblage of lawyers and public officials at the Royal Geographic Society on April 24, 1942, his reference to the opponents of that draft did not include this group.[87] To be sure, they tried to make themselves felt again, but that was in the final stages of the legislative process, when the adoption of the new code was already a foregone conclusion.

Of the three successive committees of modern-law experts set up to consider the new code, the first, appointed in March, 1936, was disbanded within three months after it had adopted the few preliminary principles that later formed the first four articles of the code. A second committee, appointed in November, 1936, laid down the rules relating to guarantee and *shuf'ah*, or preemption, before it was dissolved in May, 1938. The third committee, appointed late in 1938 and limited for efficiency to two members, al-Sanhūri and E. Lambert of France, laid down the bulk of the draft code.[88] In April, 1942, the draft code was

[87] 'Abd al-Razzāq al-Sanhūri, Muḥāḍarah 'an Mashrū' Tanqīḥ al-Qānūn al-Madani, *al-Muḥāmāh,* vol. 22, no. 5, January, 1942, pp. 419–431.

[88] For a synopsis of the various stages the draft code went through see *al-Qānūn al Madani: Majmū'at al-A'māl al-Taḥḍīriyyah,* vol. I, Cairo, 1949, pp. 5–9. It is not entirely clear why the first committee was dissolved. The second committee was disbanded at the instigation of the Ministry of Justice, which maintained, in a memorandum dated June 16, 1938, that the first stage of codification would best be accomplished by two individuals—one Egyptian and the other

offered for comment to the legal profession through al-Sanhūri's lecture at the Royal Geographic Society.

Before going into the contents of the draft, al-Sanhūri answered the charges of two groups of critics. One group had maintained that the old code was in need only of minor revisions here and there for adjustment to modern needs, and against this charge al-Sanhūri marshaled the arguments outlined in his earlier article. The second group admitted the need for recodification but expressed the fear that World War II, which was then in progress, would change the patterns of civilization to such an extent that the new code would find itself in further need of revision after the war. Al-Sanhūri pointed out that codes in other countries had withstood wars and revolutions, and that the draft had anticipated and allowed for the socialistic tendencies that were expected to follow the war by striking a balance between the freedom of the individual and the interest of the group, with emphasis on the "social function" of property.[89]

The draft code, al-Sanhūri said, was derived from twenty civil codes representing countries in Europe, Asia, Africa, and the Americas; from the jurisprudence of the Egyptian courts; and from the *sharī'ah,* along the lines he had suggested in his article on the subject. As it followed the *sharī'ah,* he asserted, the draft code tended toward objectiveness, like the Germanic codes, instead of the subjectiveness characteristic of the codes of Latin countries. The Germanic codes were chiefly concerned with the outwardly manifested will of the parties in determining an obligation, whereas the Latin codes inquired into the personal intention of the parties, and even a nonapparent will was given force in such determination. Other general principles adapted from the *sharī'ah* concerned the abuse of rights, the responsibility of young persons of imperfect understanding, the transfer of debt, and the principle of unforeseeable circumstances. In addition, many new individual rules were taken from the *sharī'ah* to

foreign—rather than by a committee, and that a committee could criticize the draft code when it was completed.

[89] Al-Sanhūri, Muḥāḍarah, pp. 419–421, 430.

supplement the previous *sharī'ah* provisions pertaining to leases of *waqfs* and agricultural lands, sale during death-sickness, fraud, option of inspection, easements, prescription, capacity, preemption, etc.[90] Further, the principles of the *sharī'ah* were made a general source of law in cases where no specific text of the code or usage was found applicable.[91]

For three years the draft code was up for comment. In 1945 a five-man committee headed by al-Sanhūri studied all the comments and proposals, introduced some revisions, and prepared the draft for legislative action. When the parliament took it up, the new code faced its most serious challenge in a specially created Senate study committee. In March, 1948, while the draft code was under consideration by the committee, a group formed by Muḥammad Ṣādiq Fahmi, a counselor at the Court of Cassation, and consisting mostly of Azharite professors of the four orthodox schools, circulated among the members of the Senate a special issue of *al-Muḥāmāh* in which the draft code was bitterly attacked. The charges seem inconsistent. On one hand, it was maintained that the old code, which, with some exceptions, had been based on French law, was in need only of some modification here and there, and that it was only right and proper to preserve the "legal culture" already accruing to Egypt. On the other hand, it was maintained that should a complete recodification be allowed, such recodification should be based on the *sharī'ah.* Perhaps the composition of the group—secular lawyers trained in the French legal tradition and professors of Islamic law at al-Azhar—was responsible for this inconsistency. The special issue was furthermore prefaced by a statement signed by four other members of the Court of Cassation which generally supported the charges, except that Ḥasan Ismā'īl al-Huḍaybi (who later became the head of the Muslim Brotherhood) recorded the reservation that all legislation should be based on the Koran.[92]

[90] Al-Sanhūri, Muḥāḍarah, pp. 426–428.

[91] Article 1, paragraph 2, of the new code.

[92] *Al-Muḥāmāh,* March, 1948, pp. 4–7 and insert before p. 3.

Faced with such oposition to the draft code, the Senate committee convened a general session on May 30, 1948, to which it invited judges and lawyers representing the Court of Cassation, the Cairo court of appeal, the mixed courts, the National Bar Association, and the Law School of Cairo University to give testimony. It is significant that none of the professors of the *sharīʿah* from either al-Azhar or the Cairo Law School were present. The session, which lasted for a few days, revealed the ephemeral nature of the opposition in the face of the single-mindedness of al-Sanhūri, who was then Minister of Education, in pushing the draft to completion, and in the face of his truly phenomenal knowledge of both the *sharīʿah* and comparative jurisprudence.

Some arguments advanced against the draft require more than passing notice. The argument that there was no need for a complete recodification has already been discussed, and most of those present at the session seemed to favor recodification. A more serious question was the multiplicity of sources of the draft and the consequent necessity of referring to twenty-odd foreign codes for the understanding of the "historical source" of a rule in order to arrive at a cogent legal solution to a given problem.[93] Al-Sanhūri met this argument with the assertion that three-fourths or four-fifths of the rules were derived from the old code and the jurisprudence of the Egyptian courts and that, in any case, "the legal provisions in the draft have an existence independent of the sources from which they were taken."[94] Finally, the question was resolved by a statement, prepared by the committee and read to the Senate:[95]

> First, that the great majority of the rules of the draft code were derived from the old code and from the jurisprudence of the Egyptian courts developed over a period of seventy

[93] See the remarks of M. Sādiq Fahmi and M. Kāmil Malash at the committee meetings in *al-Qānūn al-Madani,* pp. 70, 95.

[94] *Al-Qānūn al-Madani,* pp. 70–71.

[95] *Al-Qānūn al-Madani,* pp. 116–117.

years, that this jurisprudence was the source to which reference should be made when interpreting the new code, and that the "foreign sources" were utilized in this connection only for the purpose of arriving at a more felicitous formula when codifying;

Second, that the *sharī'ah* should be referred to when interpreting rules derived from it; and

Third, that the few rules which were derived from foreign codes relating to new subjects were formulated in such a way as to be consonant with the Egyptian environment and usages, that, therefore, they were divorced from their sources and acquired an independent existence, and that the jurisprudence of the courts should be referred to when interpreting them.

The question of utilization of the *sharī'ah* in the draft code occupied a sizable part of the committee's time. Fahmi and his supporters among the Azharite *ulema* had insisted that the *sharī'ah* alone should form the basis for any recodification. They had even published in the same special issue of *al-Muḥāmāh* a sample draft of the law of contracts purportedly based on the *sharī'ah* as proof that all branches of civil law could be so based.[96] In the committee meetings Fahmi brought up the subject repeatedly, although there did not seem to be many in support of his position. In fact, Ḥāmid Zaki of the Cairo Law School termed even the provision that would make the *sharī'ah* a source of law in the absence of any specific provision in the code or precedent of usage a kind of "*fantaisie.*" In answer to Zaki's position the chairman, M. M. al-Wakīl, pointed out that the neglect of the *sharī'ah* would cause public indignation, and al-Sanhūri added that the *sharī'ah* was preferable to the principles of equity and natural law as a reference because it was more precise. As for the position of Fahmi and his *ulema* supporters, al-Sanhūri reviewed the provisions that had been derived from the *sharī'ah* and insisted that had it been possible to derive more, he would

[96] *Al-Muḥāmāh,* March, 1948, pp. 28–102.

have gladly done so. He then took up the sample draft of the law of contracts prepared by the Fahmi group and demonstrated, principle by principle, that although the sample draft purported to be based on the *sharī'ah,* it was in point of fact based on modern codes. "If it were true," he declared, "that the provisions in the Ṣādiq sample draft—which agree with the provisions of the draft code—were *sharī'ah* rules, then we would have been justified in claiming *sharī'ah* origin for the provisions of the draft code itself, and would have avoided the charges he has proferred against it."[97]

After lengthy deliberation the committee approved the draft code with minor modifications. It is significant that one of the changes, approved unanimously, was the deletion of a provision for a *sharī'ah* type of sale called *bay' bi-al-wafā',* or sale with the right of redemption. The committee had found that this type of sale was a devious means of effecting a mortgage and had often resulted in divesting the vendor of his property for a very low price.[98]

In the Senate chamber only one senator, 'Abd al-Wahhāb Ṭal'at, raised the question of whether the *sharī'ah* had been sufficiently utilized in drawing up the code. Otherwise, the report of the special committee was enthusiastically received.[99] On October 15, 1949, the day the mixed courts and the consular courts came to an end, the draft code became the Egyptian Civil Code.

The new code shows to a remarkable extent the successful fusion of Western and Islamic elements so apparent in many aspects of Egyptian life. It is considerably more Islamic than the old one; even so, there has been some insistent clamoring for a return to the *sharī'ah.* The Muslim Brotherhood, until its suppression in October, 1954, continued to advocate basing all laws on the Koran and the *sunnah.*[100] Muḥammad Yūsuf Mūsa, a professor of Islamic law at the Law School of Cairo University,

[97] *Al-Qānūn al-Madani,* pp. 88–93.
[98] *Al-Qānūn al-Madani,* p. 137.
[99] *Al-Qānūn al-Madani,* pp. 159–167.
[100] See, for example, 'Awdah, *al-Islām wa-Awḍā'una.*

called for a serious comparative study of Islamic law in order to make it "the first basis for modern laws."[101] Even al-Sanhūri declared in a private interview that of the Egyptian, Syrian, Libyan, and Iraqi civil codes, of which he was the chief architect, the Iraqi code was nearest his heart because it was more Islamic and therefore a better model for a unified code.[102] The future may hold a wider scope for the interaction of the *sharī'ah* with modern laws.

[101] See his article, Fiqh al-Ṣaḥābah wa-al-Tābi'īn, *al-Qānūn wa-al-Iqtiṣād,* vol. 23, nos. 3, 4, September–December, 1953, p. 373.

[102] Sanhūri said further: "After working on the Egyptian code, which represents the pick of world codes, I worked on the Iraqi code. I would compare the Majallah, which was in force in Iraq, with the Egyptian code. If I found a Majallah article suitable I would take it as is, or after making it more refined in the light of the Egyptian code. Of course, the gaps were filled from the Egyptian code, and the latter's model was followed in the arrangement of the material." Interview in March, 1962.

CHAPTER SEVEN

summary and epilogue

The rise of lawyers to a dominant position in Egypt and their influence in many aspects of the life of the country during the first half of this century was in essence a facet of the process of westernization that had begun in Egypt with the Napoleonic invasion. The influence of new Western concepts led Egyptian lawyers to propagate Western-born doctrines of constitutionality, rule of law, and progressive nationalism and moved them toward a liberal outlook on many aspects of national life.

The reforms for which they were responsible did not stem from the political or legal background of Egypt. From the early Islamic period until the rule of Ismā'īl Pasha and the establishment of the mixed courts, there had been little in Egyptian history that was conducive to the emergence of an independent legal system with a vigorous body of men capable of establishing and maintaining a rule of law. The *ulema*, it is true, considered themselves the guardians and interpreters of the *sharī'ah*. However, the *sharī'ah* was constantly viewed as an ideal system of law, to be venerated irrespective of its practical applicability; hence important segments of the law escaped its jurisdiction and that of the men who applied it. What is more, the *sharī'ah* had never developed the necessary procedures or writs that would bring the prince or executive power to account for actions committed outside the law. Throughout Islamic history the judiciary, composed chiefly of *ulema,* exercised its functions as a result of delegation by the executive power and was therefore dependent upon it. Although there were some individual judges whose dedication to *sharī'ah* principles gained them hallowed positions in Islamic legal history, the situation was hardly conducive to an independent legal system.

Matters were not appreciably better even during the period of Muḥammad 'Ali and his successors, despite the efforts to secularize and modernize the state machinery. In this period of experimentation in judicial organization, rough-and-ready justice on the part of administrative officers, and abject submission of the judicial tribunals to the will, or rather, the caprice, of the pasha or his administrative officers, it was too soon to hope for a rule of law with its concomitant of an efficient and just legal system supported by a growing body of judges and lawyers aware of their role in the development of society. The 'Alawite period, as we have seen, was not completely sterile in this regard. It marked the beginning of modern legal thinking and education, translations of French codes into Arabic, codification of a variety of laws, and widespread legal knowledge among the people—all necessary elements for facilitating the later developments of the mixed and national courts.

The mixed courts, established in 1876, were, more than any other factor, responsible for the emergence of an impartial administration of justice and, by extension, the legal profession which played such a prominent role in the modernization of Egypt. The first effect of these courts was, of course, the unification of jurisdiction, with the result that litigants began to be cognizant of the court that might have to adjudicate the issue between them. Further, the uniformity of jurisdiction contributed materially to the idea of a universally applicable law. Another intimately related effect was the greater standing and prestige of judges, who in Egypt had traditionally been the lackeys of the executive power or its agents. The new judges nominated by the foreign powers not only received high salaries, but their discipline rested in their own hands as a group, thus enabling them to achieve an independence unsurpassed by any other judiciary. Furthermore, the judiciary of the mixed courts was able to demonstrate that no strongholds of privilege, including the private estates of the Khedive of Egypt, were immune in the satisfaction of judgments. Finally, the extensive work in codifying a body of laws for these courts did much to bring about greater certainty concerning the laws applicable in various situations.

In this new legal atmosphere all factors pointed to the emergence of a new class of able lawyers. The high educational standards of the European judges necessitated a similar legal education for the professional pleaders in their courts. Moreover, the ethical standards set by the new judges put a premium on lawyers who knew their law and were able to persuade their judges by legal argument, rather than on the *wukalā'* of bygone days, who had mastered the science of intercession and influence peddling. Thus the Cairo Law School flourished first under the guidance of foreign jurists and later under that of extremely able Egyptian jurists. A French school of law was established in 1890 under the auspices of the French government.[1] Many students also headed abroad, particularly to France, to study law, thus helping to integrate Egyptian legal tradition with that of the Continent.

With the establishment of the national courts in 1883, the concepts and procedures that had been developed by the mixed courts were given wider scope by their extension to strictly "na-

[1] For an account of this school see J. Y. Brinton, *The Mixed Courts of Egypt*, New Haven, Conn., 1930, pp. 273–275.

tive" issues, cases among Egyptians. This development gave rise to a fairly large group of lawyers and jurists whose professional interests depended upon the elucidation and application of the new laws. Since this entailed addressing themselves to public issues, many of them became public figures. Their general position on these issues, both individually and as a group, was a liberal and progressive one, and as a result of their involvement in matters of constitutionality and the rule of law, they became public champions of these concepts. With the establishment of the National Bar Association in 1912 the stature of the legal profession grew. The bar not only defended the rights and privileges of lawyers *vis-à-vis* the courts and the Council of Ministers, thus strengthening the concept of the right to defense in the face of authority, but it became a power to be reckoned with in the nationalist struggle and in the political process generally. Its example was followed by the *sharī'ah* lawyers, who organized a bar of their own to safeguard their rights and privileges, even though such an institution was foreign to the *sharī'ah*. This bar, however, never attained the same prestige and influence.

The secular and modern lawyers came to the fore when the old military and Azharite leadership, fell into discredit and became ineffectual following the ill-starred 'Arābi revolt. The internationalization of the Egyptian question in the aftermath of the British occupation called for the emergence of a new kind of leadership, one oriented to political action and able to establish extensive contacts in Europe in order to present the Egyptian problem to world public opinion. Such leadership was supplied by the rising generation of young lawyers, some of whom were key figures in the history of the nationalist struggle for independence from the beginning of the century to the Anglo-Egyptian treaty of 1936. The National Bar Association also played a leading role in this struggle, particularly in the rebellion of 1919. One prominent lawyer suggested facetiously that the lawyers had changed the designation "the Egyptian question" (*al-mas'alah al-Miṣriyyah*) to "the Egyptian case (or lawsuit)" (*al-qaḍiyyah al-Miṣriyyah*) in asserting that they alone had the right and the qualifications to deal with it.[2] In any event, after the complete independence of Egypt in 1936, lawyers habitually filled a considerable number of the seats in the Chamber of Deputies, the Senate, and the Council of Ministers.

The participation of lawyers in nationalist activities was paralleled by their generally liberal attitudes concerning many phases of national life. In the first quarter of the century training in law constituted the chief "liberal education" available to Egyptian students, with a resultant emphasis on individual rights and liberal causes in many of the situations in which lawyers, individually or as a group, took a stand. Nowhere was this liberalism more manifest than in the defense of the 1923 Constitution against both royal interference and encroachment by the Council of Ministers. When the draft of the Constitution was being pushed to completion King Fuad attempted by various means to amend provisions which he thought detracted from his regal powers, but the furor raised in the press by the legal profession forced the government to accept the Constitution unamended. In 1928 the bar again demonstrated itself as a force for constitutionality in vehemently protesting the suspension of the Constitution and rule of the country by decree. Two years later, when Premier Ismāʿīl Ṣidqi Pasha abolished the Constitution and substituted a much less liberal one, he took the precaution of forcibly preventing the convening of the general assembly of the bar, to prevent it from taking action. In 1948 and 1952, on the two occasions martial law was decreed and the government took advantage of its arbitrary power to curb or stifle any opposition, the general assembly of the bar demanded in no uncertain terms that the martial law be lifted.

The consistent stand of the legal profession for constitutionality and rule of law undoubtedly stemmed not only from educational background and an interest in functioning in a society that could guarantee fundamental human rights, but also from the natural desire to protect its professional interests. In

[2] Maḥmūd Kāmil, *Yawmiyyāt Muḥāmi Miṣri,* Cairo, 1944, p. 15.

many of the conflicts between the bar association and the Council of Ministers or the judiciary the ultimate issue, from the standpoint of the bar, was self-protection and resistance to any encroachment upon its rights or the rights of its members. This very goal of self-protection, however, gave a fillip to the rule of law on two scores. The fact that the bar had to justify its stand solely in terms of the rule of law afforded wider propagation of this concept. Moreover, the bar's victories imparted greater independence both to it and to its individual members in the performance of their function in the judicial process.

There is no doubt that Egypt's lawyers believed themselves to be the holders of a mission for the advancement of society as well as the champions of individual rights. In a survey the author conducted among seventy advocates in Cairo in 1958—six years after the army revolt—94 percent still believed that lawyers had "a noble mission." They indicated the nature of this mission, in descending order of preference, as "upholding of justice and human rights," "diffusion of legal knowledge and sociopolitical consciousness among the people," "serving public interest," "upholding of freedom generally and of freedom of thought in particular," "defending national rights," "raising the standards of values and ethics," and "upholding an individual's right to defense." It is interesting to note that lawyers, who had occupied some of the most important positions in the Egyptian governments and parties, still cast themselves in the role of leaders despite the eclipse they had suffered at the hands of the military regime.

In matters of legal reform the lawyers as a group showed the same spirit of liberalism. The most important of these issues was the unification of the court system. The multiplicity and uncertainty of jurisdiction among the mixed courts, the national courts, and the religious-community courts delayed and often defeated justice. Moreover, the continued existence of the mixed courts was a blow to Egyptian national pride, and the coexistence of the *millah* courts and the national courts was viewed as a divisive factor in the national ranks. The sustained campaign conducted by the legal profession against the mixed courts resulted in their complete demise in 1949. Unification of the *millah* and national courts was vehemently demanded by progressive lawyers in the face of strong opposition by conservative elements and vested interests, but had to await a strong-arm measure taken by Nasser's government. By January 1, 1956, Egypt had a single secular legal system which had jurisdiction over all persons and all justiciable issues in the country.

In the fields of family law and *waqf* endowments progressive lawyers constantly clamored for the correction of abuses pertaining to the standing of married women, the tying up of property in perpetuity, and the rules of inheritance and bequests. Some measure of reform was effected on these scores despite the cries that the *sharīʿah* was being forsaken, but family, as distinguished from charitable, *waqfs* were also not abolished until the advent of the revolutionary regime.

In the matter of reform of the civil law most lawyers seemed to want a new civil code based on positive or comparative law instead of on the *sharīʿah,* or traditional religious law.[3] However, several factors, foremost among which was national pride, dictated that a new civil code should include the *sharīʿah* to the utmost limit compatible with the requirements of present-day circumstances and practical considerations. The result was a successful fusion of Islamic and Western elements in a modern code that did not seriously offend religious and national sensibilities.

Because of the nature of their profession, the interests of Western-oriented and secular lawyers were bound up with those of the commercial elements of the upper-middle class and the landowning class. The combination of such elements formed a leadership that was modern in outlook and mildly reformist in aspirations. This leadership, royal power, and foreign influence

[3] In the 1958 survey of seventy lawyers in Cairo only fifteen of them (21.4 percent) preferred to have the *sharīʿah* as the only source of legislation, and most of these were found to have come from very modest or extremely traditional backgrounds.

(primarily British) resulted in a counterbalancing three-cornered power situation which produced a sufficiently stable milieu for parliamentary rule. However, for reasons which lie beyond the scope of this work, the leadership was unable to withstand the stresses of rapid modernization, and it gave way to the only coherent and competent force in the country, the army.[4]

When the army revolt broke out in July, 1952, lawyers were ambivalent toward the new regime. On October 3, at the first meeting of the general assembly of the bar after the revolution, the president, while voicing his support for the "blessed new movement," called on the authorities to release all the lawyers who had been put under arrest.[5] The reduction by the authorities at about this time of the government's yearly grant to the lawyers' provident fund from 10,000 to £E5,000 might have been a result of the general tightening of finances, but it could also have been an indication of the rough course ahead for the relations between the bar and the authorities.[6] Yet somehow lawyers held tenaciously to their image as the leaders of society and seemed to be awaiting an opportunity to resume this role. That opportunity was not long in coming.

In the early part of 1954 it became apparent that a showdown between President Naguib (Najīb) and Colonel Nasser ('Abd al-Nāṣir), the Deputy Prime Minister, was inevitable. Naguib was willing to cooperate with the old political parties and to call for parliamentary elections, whereas Nasser felt that such a course would bring the corrupt old elements back to

[4] For a discussion of these reasons see Manfred Halpern, *The Politics of Social Change in the Middle East and North Africa*, Princeton, N.J., 1963, pp. 41–78, 251–280; Morroe Berger, *The Arab World Today*, New York, 1964, pp. 361–369.

[5] *Minutes of the General Assembly of the National Bar Association*, part II, pp. 176–174.

[6] *Minutes*, part II, pp. 161–160. The board, in a report presented to the general assembly on December 26, 1952, voiced its conviction that the yearly government grant should, rather than being decreased, be increased to £E30,000 in lieu of the legal-aid cases the members of the bar were handling free of charge. The request went unanswered.

power. In the ensuing struggle Nasser came out on top, but not before the constitutionally minded elements in the country, which had hoped to restore parliamentary government, were forced to show their hand. On March 26, 1954, when talk was in the air of an early transfer of power to a civilian government (presumably against the wishes of Nasser), the general assembly of the bar held an extraordinary meeting to put its weight behind that course of action and to air its views on other related aims. It is indicative of the importance attached to the meeting that, although several previous meetings had been unable to muster a simple quorum of a few score, 436 members were present at this one.[7]

The meeting was a turbulent one, with a display of feelings that appear to have been released only when there was a division in the Revolutionary Command Council. Most of the meeting was devoted to a speech by 'Umar 'Umar, the president of the bar, whose announcement of the bar's demands was applauded by the members in a vehement and uproarious manner. Among the demands were the release of all political prisoners, regardless of their political beliefs, the abolishment of martial law and all laws which restricted personal freedom or the freedom of the press, the restoration of parliamentary life, the preparation of election lists, and the setting up of a neutral civilian government to supervise the elections. With reference to the army and its relation to the new order, 'Umar said:[8]

[7] The record of this meeting is in *Minutes*, part II, pp. 87–83.

[8] *Minutes*, part II, p. 85. It might appear that the forthright language used by the president of the bar was injudicious in view of the fact that the army was still in control and could therefore dictate its will, but at that time there were powerful forces backing the bar's position. Naguib, who had resigned and been reinstated, was for the return of parliamentary life, and so was 'Abd al-Razzāq al-Sanhūri, who headed the Council of State and, on account of his stand, was attacked on March 29 by a mob instigated by some army elements. In addition, the intellectuals, government employees, the press, and the powerful student body of the Cairo universities, who held a massive demonstration on March 31 against the military regime, also advocated the re-

> The country, while expressing its gratitude to the courageous army [for doing away with the corrupt monarchy], desires to preserve it for the task of defense so that nothing will distract it from that glorious duty. Such a desire, as well as the interest of Egypt and that of the army itself, require it that it go back to its barracks. . . . As a result, and in preparation for the return to normal conditions, public interest requires that the Revolutionary Command Council terminate its duties today.

He called further for the adoption by the board of the bar, in consultation with some other prominent lawyers, of a national covenant, to be subscribed to by all national elements, delineating the bases of sound parliamentary life. 'Umar's demand that the army go back to its barracks was reiterated by Muḥammad Ṣalāḥ al-Dīn, a prominent lawyer and Foreign Minister in the former Wafdist government, on the general principle that the army should not interfere in politics.[9]

Nasser's victory in the power struggle with Naguib brought to an end these dreams of restoring a representative government.[10] The minutes of the bar broke off with the March, 1954, meeting and did not resume until February, 1958. Law 709 for the year 1954 (issued September 23, 1954) dissolved the board of the bar, suspended all elections, and provided for the appointment of a new board by the Minister of Justice. The new

---

turn of constitutional government. It looked as though the movement would succeed, but pressure by Nasser and his supporters in the army had already had its effect. The Revolutionary Command Council announced on March 29 that it would continue to function until the end of the transition period in January, 1956. By the middle of November President Naguib was relieved of office and Nasser's victory was complete.

[9] *Minutes,* part II, p. 83.

[10] When 'Umar 'Umar, the previous president of the bar, was overheard to say, during the tripartite attack on Egypt in November, 1956, that Nasser should consult the leading men of the country on the steps to be taken by Egypt, he was jailed for one month. Interview with 'Umar 'Umar in April, 1958.

board, to be sure, included some of the more prominent lawyers, but its independence had become a thing of the past.[11]

By 1958 the Nasser government considered the country sufficiently stable that it could allow elections to the board of the bar. However, in March of that year, about one month before the scheduled election date, a presidential decree stipulated that all nominees to the boards of professional organizations had to be members of the National Union, Egypt's only political party. Since both the teachers' association and the engineers' association had held elections to their respective boards without such a limitation, the old-guard lawyers quite reasonably concluded that the decree was aimed at them.[12] This meant, of course, that the bar would henceforth be entrusted to "cooperative" elements and that the National Union would completely control it. Small wonder, then, that by 1962, when the author visited the National Bar Association, he was informed by its secretariat that all members had been voted in as members of the National Union, reconstituted as the Arab Socialist Union.

The government's suspicion of lawyers in general was not limited to the National Bar Association; it seems also to have embraced all law graduates. In previous years graduates of the Law School had found comparatively ready employment in the various government bureaus, but with the Nasser government this situation changed. In the words of Yaḥya Riyāḍ Sallām, deputy director of the Civil Service Commission: "The present regime is military; it intends to expedite matters quickly. Lawyers set up all sorts of limitations and reservations in their work; thus they are not very much in demand. The demand now is for the graduates of the School of Commerce."[13] The anti-

[11] The new president of the bar, the lawyer-historian 'Abd al-Raḥmān al-Rāfi'i, was somewhat apologetic in speaking to the author in January, 1958, about his being *appointed* to his office. Al-Sanhūri, in an interview in March, 1962, sharply criticized Rāfi'i for accepting that post.

[12] Interview with 'Umar 'Umar, April, 1958.

[13] Interview in January, 1958.

lawyer propaganda actually became so bad that law graduates, both in and out of government, formed an association to defend their rights to government jobs.[14]

The socialization measures adopted by the new regime had further adverse effects on the interests of lawyers. With the breakup of the big estates, the abolishment of private *waqfs* which encompassed extensive areas of land, and the nationalization of the large industrial and commercial companies, the really lucrative legal retainers disappeared. Many prominent lawyers were forced to join the various government organizations that manage these estates or companies as legal advisers, forfeiting their independent status and becoming government employees dependent on a salary. Thus the Egyptian legal profession, the leaders of society, the upholders of constitutionality and rule of law, and the supporters of liberal causes, were reduced to the status of legal technicians. Nevertheless, the rule of law they helped establish continues—with the exception of political freedoms—to be the guiding principle of the Egyptian legal system.[15]

[14] Interview with Kamāl al-Jarf in April, 1958. Al-Jarf, a law graduate and head of the Tax Bureau of the Ministry of Finance, was the organizer of this association.

[15] See the resolutions of the general assembly of the United Arab Republic judges, adopted in Cairo, March 28, 1968, wherein the rule of law and the independence of the judiciary were reiterated as necessary elements for strengthening the internal social order of the country. *Majallat al-Quḍāh,* vol. 1, no. 2, pp. 3–8.

glossary

'ālimiyyah: diploma of al-Azhar University
bayʿ bi-al-wafā': sale with the right of redemption
Copts: a Christian sect
dīwān: council
al-Dīwān al-ʿĀli: the Sublime Council
Dīwān al-Wāli: the Governor's Council
fatwa: legal opinion of a jurist
feddan: Egyptian acre (1.038 U.S. acres)
Ḥanafi: one of the four orthodox schools of law
Ḥanbali: one of the four orthodox schools of law
Ḥisbiyyah Councils: Courts of Wards
ḥiyal: legal devices
ʿiddah: period of retirement for a woman before remarriage
ijmāʿ: consensus of scholarly opinions
ijtihād: process of deducing new rules from the legal sources by the exercise of human reason
Jamʿiyyat al-Ḥaqqāniyyah: the Council of Justice
ketkhuda: chief executive officer
Majlis al-Mashūra: the Consultative Council
Māliki: one of the four orthodox schools of law
mudīr: administrative officer
mufti: jurisconsult
muḥāmūn: advocates, lawyers (sing. *muḥāmi*)
qāḍi: judge, particularly Islamic-law judge

qāḍi 'askar: originally chief military judge, later chief judge of a country or province

qiyās: analogy

Shāfi'i: one of the four orthodox schools of law

sharī'ah: Islamic law

shaykh: a religious scholar, graduate of al-Azhar University

sunnah: traditions of the Prophet Muḥammad

sunni: orthodox

sūrah: chapter of the Koran

ulema: Muslim religious scholars

wafd: delegation

waqf: dedication of property in perpetuity.

Family *waqf:* a *waqf* for the benefit of one's family primarily, and secondarily of a charitable object

Charitable *waqf:* a *waqf* for the benefit of a charity

wukalā': legal representatives, advocates, attorneys (sing. *wakīl*)

Egyptian premiers from independence to the army revolt 1922 *to* 1952

March 1, 1922–November 29, 1922	'Abd al-Khāliq Tharwat (Independent)
November 30, 1922–February 5, 1923	Muḥammad Tawfīq Nasīm (Independent)
February 5, 1922–March 15, 1923	Office vacant
March 15, 1923–January 27, 1924	Yaḥya Ibrāhīm (Independent)
January 28, 1924–November 24, 1924	Sa'd Zaghlūl (Wafd)
November 24, 1924–June 7, 1926	Aḥmad Zīwar (Independent)
June 7, 1926–April 21, 1927	'Adli Yegen (Coalition: Wafd and Liberal Constitutionalist)

April 26, 1927–March 16, 1928	ʻAbd al-Khāliq Tharwat (Coalition: Wafd and Liberal Constitutionalist)
March 17, 1928–June 25, 1928	Muṣṭafa al-Naḥḥās (Coalition: Wafd and Liberal Constitutionalist)
June 27, 1928–October 2, 1929	Muḥammad Maḥmūd (Coalition: Liberal Constitutionalist and Unionist)
October 3, 1929–December 31, 1929	ʻAdli Yegen (Independent)
January 1, 1930–June 19, 1930	Muṣṭafa al-Naḥḥās (Wafd)
June 20, 1930–September 27, 1933	Ismāʻīl Ṣidqi (Independent; then Populist and Unionist)
September 27, 1933–November 14, 1934	ʻAbd al-Fattāḥ Yaḥya (Populist)
November 15, 1934–January 30, 1936	Muḥammad Tawfīq Nasīm (Independent)
January 30, 1936–May 9, 1936	ʻAli Māhir (Independent)
May 10, 1936–December 30, 1937	Muṣṭafa al-Naḥḥās (Wafd)
December 30, 1937–August 12, 1939	Muḥammad Maḥmūd (Coalition: Liberal Constitutionalist and others)
August 18, 1939–June 27, 1940	ʻAli Māhir (Independent and Saʻdist)
June 28, 1940–November 14, 1940	Ḥasan Ṣabri (Saʻdist, Liberal Constitutionalist, National, and Independent)

November 15, 1940–February 4, 1942	Ḥusayn Sirri (Liberal Constitutionalist and Independent, then Sa'dist also)
February 6, 1940–October 8, 1944	Muṣṭafa al-Naḥḥās (Wafd)
October 9, 1944–February 24, 1945	Aḥmad Māhir (Sa'dist, Liberal Constitutionalist, Kutlah Wafdiyyah, National)
February 24, 1945–February 15, 1946	Maḥmūd Fahmi al-Nuqrāshi (same as previous coalition)
February 17, 1946–December 9, 1946	Ismā'īl Ṣidqi (Independent, then Sa'dist also)
December 9, 1946–December 28, 1948	Maḥmūd Fahmi al-Nuqrāshi (Sa'dist and Liberal Constitutionalist)
December 28, 1948–July 25, 1949	Ibrāhīm 'Abd al-Hādi (Sa'dist, Liberal Constitutionalist, and Independent)
July 26, 1949–January 12, 1950	Ḥusayn Sirri (Coalition of all parties; then a "neutral" government)
January 12, 1950–January 27, 1952	Muṣṭafa al-Naḥḥās (Wafd)
January 27, 1952–March 1, 1952	'Ali Māhir (Independent)
March 1, 1952–June 28, 1952	Najīb al-Hilāli (Independent)
July 2, 1952–July 22, 1952	Ḥusayn Sirri (Independent)
July 22, 1952–July 23, 1952	Najīb al-Hilāli (Independent)

bibliography

'Abd al-Wahhāb, Ṣalāḥ al-Dīn: *Mudawwanat al-Aḥwāl al-Shakhṣiyyah li-ghayr al-Muslimīn* (*Digest of the Personal-status Law for Non-Muslims*), Cairo, 1959.

Abu-Lughod, Ibrahim: *Arab Rediscovery of Europe*, Princeton, N.J., 1963.

Abu Zahrah, Muḥammad: Mashrū' al-Qānūn al-Khāṣṣ bi-Taqyīd al-Ṭalāq wa-Ta'addud al-Zawjāt (Bill for Limiting Divorce and Polygamy), *al-Qānūn wa-al-Iqtiṣād*, vol. 15, January–March, 1945, pp. 125–184.

Adams, Charles Clarence: *Islam and Modernism in Egypt*, London, 1933.

Aḥmad, Jamāl M.: *The Intellectual Origins of Egyptian Nationalism*, London, 1960.

'Allūbah, Muḥammad 'Ali: *Mabādi' fi al-Siyāsah al-Miṣriyyah* (*Principles of Egyptian Politics*), Cairo, 1942.

Anderson, James Norman Dalrymple: *Islamic Law in the Modern World*, New York, 1959.

Anderson, James Norman Dalrymple: Recent Developments in Sharī'a Law, *The Muslim World*, vols. 40–42, 1950–1952.

Anṭūn, Farīd: *Mustaqbal al-Qaḍā' fi Miṣr* (*The Future of the Judiciary in Egypt*), Cairo, 1929.

al-'Aqqād, 'Abbās Maḥmūd: *Sa'd Zaghlūl*, Cairo, 1936.

'Āṣim, Maḥmūd: *al-Murāfa'āt fi Ashhar al-Qaḍāya* (*Proceedings of the Most Famous Trials*), 2 vols., Cairo, 1933–1935.

'Awdah, 'Abd al-Qādir: *al-Islām wa-Awḍā'una al-Qānūniyyah* (*Islam and Our Legal Circumstance*), Cairo, 1951.

'Azzām, H. M.: al-Waṣiyyah al-Wājibah (Obligatory Bequest), *al-Muḥāmāh*, vol. 37, April, 1957, pp. 1046–1060.

Badawi, ʻAbd al-Ḥamīd: Athar al-Imtiyāzāt fi al-Qaḍā' wa-al-Tashrī' fi Miṣr (Capitulations, the Judiciary, and Law in Egypt), *al-Kitāb al-Dhahabi lil-Maḥākim al-Ahliyyah* (*The Golden Book of the National Courts*), vol. II, Cairo, 1938, pp. 1–61.

Badawi, ʻAbd al-Ḥamīd: La Tarikah illa ba'd Dayn (No Inheritance before Payment of Debts), *al-Muḥāmāh,* vol. 1, February–March, 1921, pp. 369–376, 433–439.

Baer, Gabriel: Tanzimat in Egypt: The Penal Code, *Bulletin of the School of Oriental and African Studies,* vol. 26, part I, 1963, pp. 29–49.

Bakhīt, Muḥammad: Tawḥīd Sinn al-Zawāj (Fixing the Age of Marriage), *al-Muḥāmāh,* vol. 4, January, 1924, pp. 399–411.

Berger, Morroe: *The Arab World Today,* New York, 1964.

Brinton, J. Y: *The Mixed Courts of Egypt,* New Haven, Conn., 1930.

Coulson, N. J.: *A History of Islamic Law,* Edinburgh, 1964.

Cromer, Evelyn Baring: *Modern Egypt,* New York, 1908.

Debs, Richard A.: *The Law of Property in Egypt* (unpublished doctoral dissertation, Princeton University, Department of Oriental Studies), Princeton, N.J., 1963.

Description de l'Égypte, vol. 18, Paris, 1826.

Fahmi, ʻAbd al-ʻAzīz: Mudhakkirāt (Memoirs), *al-Muṣawwar,* June 24, 1949.

Halpern, Manfred: *The Politics of Social Change in the Middle East and North Africa,* Princeton, N.J., 1963.

Harris, Christina Phelps: *Nationalism and Revolution in Egypt: The Role of the Muslim Brotherhood,* Palo Alto, Calif., 1967.

Haykal, Muḥammad Ḥusayn: *Tarājim Miṣriyyah wa-Gharbiyyah* (*Egyptian and Western Biographies*), Cairo, n.d.

Haykal, Muḥammad Ḥusayn, et al.: *al-Siyāsah al-Miṣriyyah wa-al-Inqilāb al-Dustūri* (*Egyptian Politics and the Constitutional Upheaval*), Cairo, 1931.

Heyworth-Dunne, J.: *An Introduction to the History of Education in Modern Egypt,* London, 1938.

al-Hilbāwi, Ibrāhīm: Rijāl al-Qaḍā' al-Rāḥilūn (Deceased Judges), *al-Kitāb al-Dhahabi lil- Maḥākim al-Ahliyyah* (*The Golden Book of the National Courts*), vol. I, Cairo, 1937.

Hourani, Albert H.: *Arabic Thought in the Liberal Age,* 1798–1939, London, 1962.

al-Ḥusayni, Isḥāq Mūsa: *The Moslem Brethren* (tr. by John F. Brown and John Racy), Beirut, 1956.

Ibn Iyās, Muḥammad ibn Aḥmad: *Badā'i' al-Zuhūr fi Waqā'i' al-Duhūr* (a history), 3 vols., Bulaq, 1893–1894.

Issawi, Charles: *Egypt at Mid-century,* London, 1954.

al-Jabarti, 'Abd al-Raḥmān: *'Ajā'ib al-Āthār fi al-Tarājim wa-al-Akhbār* (a history), 4 vols., Bulaq, 1297 A.H.

al-Jundi, 'Abd al-Ḥalīm: *al-Hilbāwi,* Cairo, n.d.

Kāmil, Maḥmūd: *Yawmiyyat Muḥāmi Miṣri* (*Memoirs of an Egyptian Advocate*), Cairo, 1944.

Kerr, Malcolm H.: *Islamic Reform: The Political and Legal Theories of Muḥammad 'Abduh and Rashīd Riḍa,* Berkeley, 1966.

Khadduri, M., and H. J. Liebesny (eds.): *Law in the Middle East,* Washington, D.C., 1955.

Khallāf, 'Abd al-Wahhāb: al-Sharī'ah al-Islāmiyyah wa-al-Shu'ūn al-Ijtimā'iyyah (Islamic Law and Social Affairs), *al-Qānūn wa-al-Iqtiṣad,* vol. 17, March, 1947, pp. 137–158.

Khānki, 'Azīz: *Aḥādīth* (*Essays*), Cairo, n.d.

Khānki, 'Azīz: *al-Maḥākim al-Mukhtaliṭah wa-al-Maḥākim al-Ahliyyah* (*The Mixed Courts and the National Courts*), Cairo, 1939.

Khānki, 'Azīz: *al-Tashrī' wa-al-Qaḍā' qabl Inshā' al-Maḥākim al-Ahliyyah* (*Law and the Judiciary before the Establishment of the National Courts*), Cairo, n.d.

Khānki, 'Aziz, and Jamīl Khānki: *al-Muḥāmāh Qadīman wa-Ḥadīthan* (*Advocacy, Old and New*), Cairo, 1940.

Lacouture, Jean, and Simonne Lacouture: *Egypt in Transition,* London, 1958.

Landau, Jacob M.: *Parliaments and Parties in Egypt,* Tel-Aviv, 1953.

League of Arab States: *Wathā'iq wa-Nuṣūṣ* (*Documents and Texts*), Cairo, 1955 et seq.

Mahmassani, S.: *Falsafat al-Tashrī' fi al-Islām,* tr. by Farhat J. Ziadeh (as *The Philosophy of Jurisprudence in Islam*), Leiden, 1961.

Majallat Majlis al-Dawlah (*Journal of the Council of State*), Cairo, 1950 et seq.

Marlowe, John: *Anglo-Egyptian Relations,* 1800–1953, London, 1954.

Minutes of the General Assembly of the National Bar Association.

Mursi, M. K.: Kulliyyat al-Ḥuqūq (The Law School), *al-Kitāb al-Dhahabi lil-Maḥakim al-Ahliyyah* (*The Golden Book of the National Courts*), vol. I, Cairo, 1937, pp. 409–432.

Mūsa, Muḥammad Yūsuf: Fiqh al-Ṣaḥābah wa-al-Tābi'īn (The Jurisprudence of the Companions and Successors), *al-Qānūn wa-al-Iqtiṣad,* vol. 23, September–December, 1953, pp. 365–450.

Osman, Amin: *Le mouvement constitutionnel en Égypte et la constitution de* 1923, Paris, 1924.

al-Rāfi'i, 'Abd al-Raḥmān: *'Aṣr Muḥammad 'Ali* (*The Age of Muḥammad Ali*), Cairo, 1947.

al-Rāfiʻi, ʻAbd al-Raḥmān: *Fi Aʻqāb al-Thawrah al-Miṣriyyah* (*The Aftermath of the Egyptian Rebellion*), 3 vols., Cairo, 1947–1951.

al-Rāfiʻi, ʻAbd al-Raḥmān: *Mudhakkirāti* (*Memoirs*), Cairo, 1952.

al-Rāfiʻi, ʻAbd al-Raḥmān: *Muḥammad Farīd*, Cairo, 1948.

al-Rāfiʻi, ʻAbd al-Raḥmān: *Muṣṭafa Kāmil*, Cairo, 1950.

al-Rāfiʻi, ʻAbd al-Raḥmān: *Thawrat Sanat* 1919 (*The Rebellion of* 1919), 2 vols., Cairo, 1946.

Report of the Judicial Adviser for the Year 1905.

Report of the Judicial Adviser for the Year 1916.

Riḍā, Muḥammad Rashīd: Madaniyyat al-Qawānīn (The Secularity of Laws), *al-Manār*, vol. 23, 1922, pp. 539–548.

Ṣabri, Muṣṭafa: Ḍarūrat Ilghāʼ al-Awqāf al-Ahliyyah (The Necessity of Abolishing Family Waqfs), *al-Muḥāmāh*, vol. 7, April, 1927, pp. 751–754.

Ṣabri, Muṣṭafa: *Iqtirāḥāt fi Ilghāʼ al-Awqāf al-Ahliyyah* (*Suggestions for Abolishing Family Waqfs*), Cairo, 1923.

Safran, Nadav: *Egypt in Search of Political Community*, Cambridge, Mass., 1961.

Ṣafwat, Aḥmad: *Iqtirāḥāt fi Iṣlāḥ Nuẓum al-Qaḍāʼ* (*Suggestions for Reforming the Courts*), Cairo, 1929.

Ṣafwat, Aḥmad: *Qaḍāʼ al-Aḥwāl al-Shakhṣiyyah lil-Ṭawāʼif al-Milliyyah* (*The Personal-status Courts of Non-Muslims*), Cairo, 1936.

Ṣafwat, Aḥmad: *Qāʻidat Iṣlāḥ Qānūn al-Aḥwāl al-Shakhṣiyyah* (*The Basis for the Reform of the Law of Personal Status*), Alexandria, 1917.

Ṣafwat, Aḥmad: The Theory of Mohammedan Law, *Journal of Comparative Legislation and International Law*, vol. 2, 1920, pp. 310–316.

al-Sanhūri, ʻAbd al-Razzāq: *Le califat: son évolution vers une société des nations orientale*, Paris, 1926.

al-Sanhūri, ʻAbd al-Razzāq: Muḥāḍarah ʻan Mashrūʻ Tanqīḥ al Qānūn al-Madani (Lecture on the Project for Revising the Civil Code), *al-Muḥāmāh*, vol. 22, January, 1942, pp. 419–431.

al-Sanhūri, ʻAbd al-Razzāq: [Obituary of] ʻAbd al-ʻAzīz Fahmi, *Majallat Majlis al-Dawlah*, vol. 2, January, 1951, pp. i–xi.

al-Sanhūri, ʻAbd al-Razzāq: al-Taʻbīr ʻan Raʼy al-Ummah (Expressing the Nation's Will), *al-Hilāl*, vol. 46, April, 1938, pp. 601–603.

al-Sanhūri, ʻAbd al-Razzāq: L'Université Égyptienne dans le Congrès International de Droit Comparé de la Haye, *al-Qānūn wa-al-Iqtiṣād*, vol. 2, 1932, pp. 289–312.

al-Sanhūri, ʻAbd al-Razzāq: *Maṣādir al-Ḥaqq fi al-Fiqh al-Islāmi* (*Sources of Rights in Islamic Law*), 5 vols., Cairo, 1954–1958.

al-Sanhūri, 'Abd al-Razzāq: Wujūb Tanqīh al-Qānūn al-Madani (The Necessity of Revising the Civil Code), *al-Qānūn wa-al-Iqtiṣād*, vol. 6, January, 1936, pp. 3–144.

al-Sanhūri, Muḥammad Aḥmad Faraj: *Majmū'at al-Qawānīn al-Miṣriyyah al-Mukhtārah min al-Fiqh al-Islāmi* (*Digest of Egyptian Laws Taken from Islamic Law*), vol. III, Cairo, 1949.

al-Sayyid, 'Abd al-Fattāḥ: La situation de la femme mariée égyptienne après douze ans de réformes legislatives, *al-Qānūn wa-al-Iqtiṣad*, vol. 2, 1932, pp. 65–82.

al-Sayyid, Aḥmad Luṭfi: Mudhakkirāt (Memoirs), *al-Muṣawwar*, September 7, 1950.

al-Sayyid, Aḥmad Luṭfi: *al-Muntakhabāt* (*Selections*), Cairo, 1945.

al-Sayyid, Aḥmad Luṭfi: *Mushkilat al-Ḥurriyyah* (*The Problem of Freedom*), Beirut, 1959.

al-Sayyid, Aḥmad Luṭfi: *Qiṣṣat Ḥayāti* (*Autobiography*) (ed. by Ṭāhir al-Ṭanāḥi), Cairo, 1960.

al-Sayyid, Aḥmad Luṭfi: *Ta'ammulāt* (*Reflections*), Cairo, 1946.

al-Sayyid, Aḥmad Luṭfi (ed.): *al-Duktūr Muḥammad Ḥusayn Haykal*, Cairo, 1958.

Schacht, Joseph: *An Introduction to Islamic Law*, London, 1964.

Schemeil, Raymond: *De la profession d'avocat près les jurisdictions mixtes d'Égypte*, Alexandria, 1936.

Sfeir, George N.: The Abolition of Confessional Jurisdiction in Egypt, *The Middle East Journal*, vol. 10, 1956, pp. 248–256.

Minutes of the Sharī'ah Bar Association, Ministry of Finance, Cairo.

al-Shayyāl, Jamāl al-Dīn Muḥammad: *Rifā'ah al-Ṭahṭāwi*, Cairo, 1945.

al-Shayyāl, Jamāl al-Dīn Muḥammad: *Tārīkh al-Tarjamah wa-al-Ḥarakah al-Thaqāfiyyah fi 'Aṣr Muḥammad 'Ali* (*History of Translation and the Cultural Movement in the Age of Muhammad Ali*), Cairo, 1951.

Shiḥātah, Shafīq: *Tārīkh Ḥarakat al-Tajdīd fi al-Nuẓum al-Qānūniyyah fi Miṣr* (*History of the Reform of Legal Institutions in Egypt*), Cairo, 1961.

Ṣidqi, Ismā'īl: *Mudhakkirāti* (Memoirs), Cairo, 1950.

Sousa, Nasīm: *The Capitulatory Regime of Turkey: Its History, Origin, and Nature*, Baltimore, Md., 1933.

al-Subki, 'Abd al-Wahhāb ibn 'Ali: *Mu'īd al-Ni'am* (ed. by David W. Wyhram), London, 1908.

Sulaymān, Muḥammad: Bi-Ayy Shar' Nuḥkam? (By What Law Are We to Be Ruled?), *L'Égypte contemporaine*, vol. 27, April, 1936, pp. 289–365.

Tyan, Emile: *Histoire de l'organisation judiciaire en pays d'Islam,* 2 vols., Paris, 1938–1943.
al-'Urābi, 'Ali Zaki: Markaz al-Wārith fi al-Qawānīn al-Miṣriyyah (The Position of the Heir in Egyptian Law), *al-Muḥāmāh,* vol. 1, November, 1920, pp. 225–237.
Zaghlūl, Aḥmad Fatḥi: *al-Muḥāmāh* (*Advocacy*), Cairo, 1900.
Zaki, Naṣīf: al-Maḥākim al-Ahliyyah wa-al-Aḥwāl al-Shakhṣiyyah (The National Courts and Personal Status), *al-Qānūn wa-al-Iqtiṣād,* vol. 4, 1934, pp. 787–832.
Zāyid, Maḥmūd Y.: *Egypt's Struggle for Independence,* Beirut, 1965.
Ziadeh, Farhat J.: Equality (*Kafā'ah*) in the Muslim Law of Marriage, *The American Journal of Comparative Law,* vol. 6, 1957, pp. 503–517.

index